ISLAS

AS

EMMA WARREN

Smith Street Books

INTRODUCTION

The Balearic Islands are home to turquoise seas, bright orange sunsets, powdery white sands, rugged mountain landscapes, colourful villages and historic towns. Although these may sound like marketing slogans targeted towards tourists who flock to the islands every year for their dose of sun, sea and sand, dig a little deeper and you will discover a unique part of the Mediterranean filled with tradition, soul and some of the finest cuisine that Spain has to offer. Over time, this paradise has been home to artists, musicians and writers; a place where fiercely passionate locals protect their heritage, identity and culture through traditional customs, food and festivals.

Situated to the east of the Spanish Iberian Peninsula and north of Algeria, the Balearics are the westernmost islands in the Mediterranean. The four main islands Mallorca, Menorca, Ibiza and Formentera, together with 164 islets and reefs, are grouped into two geographical areas: the Gymnesian Islands (Mallorca, Menorca and the smaller Cabrera) and the Pityusic Islands (Ibiza, Formentera and the uninhabited S'Espalmador). Collectively, these islands are an autonomous province of Spain, and although they have much in common with the Iberian mainland, each island has its own dialect, culture and history, particularly when it comes to cuisine.

MALLORCA

The island of Mallorca is the largest in the Balearic archipelago and its capital, Palma, also serves as the capital of the Balearic Islands. The city is a destination in its own right with narrow boulevards, historical landmarks, vibrant bars and restaurants and a busy waterfront sporting some of the biggest mega yachts you'll ever see. Beyond the city and away from the resorts lie picturesque coastal villages, spotlessly clean, sandy beaches, historic inland towns and the mountainous Serra de Tramuntana.

Throughout the year, the Mallorcan calendar is filled with 'festes' (festivals), with each town or village paying homage to their favourite saint, sinner or historical event. Streets are lined with markets and religious processions in a grand display of celebration and community. Many coastal towns celebrate Santa Carmen, the patron saint of sailors, and every year her effigy is set alight and sailed out to sea as an offering in return for a year of successful fishing.

Mallorca is an island of contrasting pleasures and although it's largely dependent on tourism, this affords it a self-sufficient, laid-back and family-focused attitude, which suits tourists and locals alike. Whichever experience you're looking for, you can be sure that the food will be good. From the top-end hotels serving elaborate seafood dishes to the rustic village cafes, bakeries and restaurants that serve local breads, ensaïmadas, sobrassada and 'herbes' (herb liqueur), your culinary experience on Mallorca will be a memorable one.

MENORCA

In contrast to Mallorca, the smaller island of Menorca has a low-key, quieter existence. Rich in indigenous flora and fauna, it is also known for its ancient megalithic stone monuments, UNESCO biosphere nature reserve and golden, sandy beaches. As a result of repeated invasion over the last 2000 years, Menorca can attribute much of its culture to Roman, Jewish, Arabic, French and British influences. Over time, they have all left their mark on the history of the island, not least its cuisine.

The capital, Maó (Mahón in Spanish) lays claim to the origins of the most famous condiment in the world, 'mahonesa' (mayonnaise), while also being home to Mahón cheese and the popular Xoriguer Gin (both British legacies). The island is also known for its gastronomy, and on Menorca seafood reigns supreme with restaurants showcasing the daily catch of fish and shellfish. Their most famous dish is a lobster hotpot (see page 190), and if you find it on a local menu, order it, as you will be rewarded with one of the most decadent dishes throughout the whole Balearic Islands.

IBIZA

'Eivissa', as it is locally known, may be the world's number one party destination with its mix of hedonism, outrageous summer clubbing schedules and international DJs (plus some casual celebrity spotting), but Ibiza also has an introverted side. Move away from the nightclubs and crowds and you'll find stunning beaches, white-washed villages, hippy markets and legends of mysterious sirens and strange magnetic fields! In the island's interior, the down-to-earth rural community is committed to conservation and maintaining the 'Ibicenco' (Ibizan) way of life among their modern, evolving surrounds.

Mint and fennel grow wild throughout the island and are subsequently used in popular dishes, such as the famous Ibizan mint and aniseed tart (see page 258) and moreish Lent doughnuts (see page 31). There's also a Christmas brioche (see page 37), which is traditionally dipped in an unusual meat sauce and eaten as dessert, along with other dishes, such as hunter's rice (see page 200) and perhaps the biggest culinary star of the island, Ibizan fish stew (see page 175).

FORMENTERA

The most southerly point of the Balearic Islands, Formentera is a true oasis. With a laid-back attitude, it is a land of sand, sea and salt flats. It is also a place of rejuvenation for travellers who make the pilgrimage there after all the fun on Ibiza gets overwhelming or boring. Protected from over-development, late-night institutions and shopping malls, Formentera has become a haven for the European boho-chic crowd. It's also family friendly, safe and relaxed; a place where you can spend the whole day shuffling between the shade of the palm trees, the beach, your boat, the bar or local restaurant. Lobster with rice, lobster with garlic, lobster salad or just plain old lobster is definitely on all the island's menus, such is the abundance of this prized shellfish. Simple salads are also always available, along with myriad types of grilled or fried fish. Refreshing fruit-based desserts also abound, or seek out a traditional 'greixonera' (Balearic pudding, see page 249) to keep up your levels of indulgence.

The Balearic Islands may be famous for their coastlines, but take a trip off the beaten path and journey inland, and you'll be rewarded with a rich landscape where centuries-old agricultural practices and cultural heritage have not been forgotten. Castles and fortresses still hold strong, surrounded by stone-walled villages and windmill-dotted fields. It is here that you'll find olive oil still being pressed in the traditional way, fruit orchards, wild-growing herbs, freely roaming chickens and pigs, and terraces for irrigation left by the Moors. So important were these island interiors that historically daughters inherited the 'worthless' real estate by the coast, while the boys inherited the fertile land. Only now it is the daughters who are rich after the onset of tourism, having sold or rented their estates to eager property developers!

By virtue of the Balearics' position in the Mediterranean Sea, many civilisations have occupied the islands at one time or another and they have all left their cultural and culinary mark. The Phoenicians, Romans, Vandals, Byzantines, Moors, Jews, French, British and, of course, the Spanish have all laid claim to this part of the Mediterranean with possession toing and froing between them. Mint and aniseed were introduced by the Moors and today both are distinctly Balearic. The eggplant (aubergine) was also introduced from the East, along with the trend of adding fruit and nuts to savoury dishes, which helped set Balearic cuisine apart from mainland Spain. From further afield, the conquistadors returned with potatoes, tomatoes and capsicums (bell peppers), and it's hard to imagine a Balearic meal without these classic ingredients.

Seasonal fishing, agriculture and horticultural farming, which were once the cornerstone of all Balearic dishes, still provide many of the ingredients used in everyday cooking with honey, lard, olive oil, pimentòn and vinegar forming the foundation of many meals. These raw goods, shared among the local community, are transformed into substantial family meals or preserved and cured in the form of charcuterie, cheese, brined olives, dried fruits, almonds, pickled fish and various condiments and conserves to last through the year.

Our journey through the Balearic Islands' rich culinary history begins in the bakery, which is also where many locals start their day. Bread is made and bought daily and might be eaten with a drizzle of olive oil and local tomatoes or with sobrassada and honey. The bakery is where you will also find the islands' culinary mascot, the ensaïmada (see page 32), along with doughnuts, festive lard cookies, savoury topped flatbreads, meaty pasties, turnovers and pastries, which are usually enjoyed with a strong morning coffee.

The Balearic home is where age-old practices for safeguarding surplus ingredients are still practised, and so Casolana (see page 52) is filled with recipes for preserving and pickling. Here, excess fruit is transformed into jams and pastes, while olives are salted and brined using local techniques and paired with indigenous island flavours. Like other Spanish regions, the Balearics have a love for preserving seafood and pickled white anchovies or mussels are regularly made at home and enjoyed as an aperitivo. These pickled delicacies also add an instant flavour hit to salads, making them excellent to have on hand when you want something quick and tasty to eat. Finally, it is customary to finish any Balearic meal with a shot of 'herbes' (see page 82) and many families will have a bottle of this moonshine digestif to share with friends and family on special occasions. It's easy to recreate at home and thoroughly worth the time to bring a little island life to your meal.

Vegetables have always been and still are a huge staple in Mediterranean cuisine, and the Balearic Islands are no exception. 'Poble', meaning 'village', takes a wander through the vegetable patch, where locals still till the earth and rely on fresh, seasonal ingredients for their daily meal. The islands' soil is ideal for growing any number of Mediterranean vegetables, from eggplants (aubergines) and tomatoes to leafy greens such as silverbeet (Swiss chard) and many other leaves that only grow on the Balearics. When it comes to cooking these ingredients, vegetables at their peak are allowed to shine and take centre stage in light suppers, hearty side dishes, substantial soups and salads.

Due to an abundance of coastlines, seafood has always been a main source of protein on the islands and it forms the backbone of the Balearic palate. Loved by tourists and locals alike, the choice of fish and shellfish is vast, and bars and restaurants will showcase the catch of the day on handwritten blackboards, enticing customers in. Seafood takes centre stage in many dishes, whether it's whole fish grilled to perfection on the barbecue or cooked slowly in a stew or paella. These Balearic feasts will probably be the most memorable meal you'll eat on the islands, especially if experienced at any one of the bustling 'xiringuito' (beach shacks) or more upmarket restaurants that sell huge platters of freshly caught shellfish. Just don't forget the allioli and wine!

Inland, 'muntanya' (see page 194) represents the provincial heartland of the Balearics, where a taste of real island life can be found. Rural villages and towns are held together by an inclusive community spirit, where neighbouring farmhouses (fincas) look out for each other and unite to preserve the land. Here, pork forms the base of many traditional dishes, especially in the production of the famous fermented sobrassada sausage (see page 216), made with that other famous Spanish ingredient, pimentòn. Lamb and poultry, once reserved for special occasions, are also frequently consumed, but always quite modestly, perhaps with the addition of seasonal vegetables, rice, fideo pasta, foraged herbs and occasionally dried fruit and nuts.

In 'postres', you will find not only classic sweet and digestive desserts to conclude a special meal, but also dishes that are eaten at festivals and shared among loved ones. Many of these Balearic desserts are steeped in history, representing long-lasting legacies of invasion and colonialism. Nougats (turróns) left by the Moors, puddings from the British and even caramels left by the French are a regular feature on many menus, all presented with a Balearic twist that might include honey, citrus or almonds.

My love for these islands began in Mallorca at the age of 21. There, in the easternmost point of Cala Ratjada, I also began my relationship with food and discovered a passion for cooking through the wonderful produce available. This experience saw me return summer after summer on new paths to discovery and adventure, and over time it became clear to me that the islands draw you in and keep you coming back, curious for more depth and knowledge about their culture and lifestyle. Living on the Balearic Islands formed some of the greatest and most memorable, formative moments of my life. There was always a new custom, quaint village, hidden cove, cosy beach or secluded bay to find, leaving me wanting more of its unique flare and sense of remoteness. It is an addictive place, where people work hard, play hard and holiday harder in the pursuit of the joys of island life and the pure art of living. Welcome!

FORN DE
PASTIS

The bakery is the window into the heart and soul of daily life on the Balearic Islands, and although the famously revered ensaïmada (see page 32) might be known as the islands' culinary symbol, there's plenty more to the baked goods in this part of Spain than these devilishly delicious iconic pastries.

Throughout Spain's autonomous Catalan-speaking communities, bakeries are known as 'forn' (oven), 'forn de pa' (bread oven), 'pastisserias' (pastry shops) or the longer, more literal version 'forn de pa I pastisserias', and you will find these establishments dotted throughout the islands, enticing you in with their array of savoury or sweet baked goods. Wandering through the old towns of Mallorca, Ibiza and Menorca, it's impossible to resist stepping inside and sampling everything from the simple breads bought fresh and eaten daily with the freshest of olive oils and maybe a little tomato, to savoury pies and turnovers and various sweet cookies, tarts and doughnuts, which are enjoyed for breakfast or morning tea with a strong coffee.

Many of these artisan establishments and their closely guarded recipes have been passed down through families, with some counting up to five generations of bakers and pastry chefs. The flourmill, once a powerful institution providing an essential commodity, remains an emblematic figure throughout the islands, but today there are very few still operational and modern grains more suited to mass production have crept into bread production. The structure and density of these baked goods have, however, remained the same and you'll find that pastries, breads and cookies are generally much harder than their French counterparts. This is perhaps partly due to the continued use of 'saïm' (lard) instead of butter, which has a higher heat point and requires a denser flour, such as baker's flour or strong flour (also known as bread flour). These harder flours provide better protection against the high moisture levels in the island air, which can lead to baked goods becoming damp and turning mouldy quickly. Potato and sweet potato are also common ingredients added to baking to help retain a spongy, fluffy texture and a crispier crust.

Believe it or not, lard has much less saturated fat than butter. If you prefer to use butter, then feel free to substitute it in equal quantities, but don't do it on account of your health. Lard will give you a much more neutral, almost savoury depth to your doughs and pastries, and it will result in a softer flavour. Using a 50/50 mix is a good compromise, but beware that the butter will dominate the flavour of the lard, which can supress the essence of these traditional Balearic favourites.

PA MORENO MALLORQUIN (PA AMB OLI)

Mallorcan rye bread

MAKES 1 LOAF

'Xeixa' is an ancient grain indigenous to the Balearic Islands, which is low in gluten and easy to digest. It has a sweet and intense nutty flavour, and the closest I have come to replicating it is to use a mix of rye and stoneground wheat flours. Traditionally, no salt is used in this bread recipe, as the salt in the island air adds a mineral component to the grain. Originally associated with peasant farmers and the rural community, it's now popular throughout the islands for its flavour and high-fibre health benefits.

This bread goes well with any recipe in this book that calls for crusty bread on the side.

400 g (14 oz) strong wholemeal (whole-wheat) stoneground flour

200 g (7 oz/2 cups) light rye flour, plus extra for dusting

1 teaspoon fine sea salt

2 teaspoons honey

2 tablespoons boiling water

300 ml (10 fl oz) mineral water, at room temperature

14 g (½ oz) dry active yeast

extra virgin olive oil spray

extra virgin olive oil, to serve

sea salt flakes, to serve

Grandma's smashed olives (see page 73), to serve (optional)

Pickled sea fennel (see page 70), to serve (optional)

Sift the flours and salt into the bowl of a stand mixer with the dough hook attached. Combine for a few seconds on low speed.

Combine the honey and boiling water in a bowl, then pour in the mineral water. Stir through the yeast and set aside to activate for 5–8 minutes.

Increase the mixer to medium speed and pour the yeast mixture into the flour. Reduce the speed to medium–low and knead for 2–3 minutes, until the dough comes together.

Dust a clean work surface with rye flour and tip out the dough. Using your hands, knead for a further 6–8 minutes, until smooth. Shape the dough into a ball and place in a large bowl lightly sprayed with oil. Spray a little oil on top of the bread, then cover with plastic wrap and set aside in a warm, draught-free spot for 1–2 hours, until risen by one-third.

Transfer the dough back to a lightly floured work surface and lightly knead for a few minutes to knock out any air bubbles. Shape the dough into a smooth, round shape, then transfer to a large square of lightly oiled baking paper and set aside, covered with a damp tea towel, for a further 1–1½ hours, until increased by another one-third.

Preheat the oven to 220°C (430°F) fan-forced. Preheat a 24 cm (9½ in) flameproof round casserole dish on the stovetop over medium heat or in the oven for 20 minutes.

Dust the top of the dough with a little rye flour and cut a few slashes into the top with a sharp knife. Carefully transfer the dough with the baking paper to the hot dish and trim any overhanging paper. Cover with a lid and bake for 30 minutes, then remove the lid and bake for a further 10 minutes or until golden brown on top and cooked through.

Remove the bread from the dish and set aside on a wire rack to cool for 20 minutes.

Serve with a little olive oil and a sprinkle of salt flakes, and some smashed olives and pickled sea fennel on the side, if you like, for an authentic island taste.

BAKERY

LLONGUET

Bread rolls

MAKES 4

The closest thing I've found to these bread rolls is the Italian 'pasta dura'. It's nearly impossible to exactly recreate local breads, as it often comes down to individual bakers and the grains they use, distinct water compositions and yeast availability. When you want to recreate that filled bocadillo, baguette or panini you ate when you were on holiday, the best way is to make your own bread to try and set the scene for the rest of the story.

This recipe is my memory of the local bread rolls sold throughout the Balearics. Every day I would eat a roll filled with Mahón cheese or jamón for a lunch on the run. It was also my go-to bread for soaking up any left-over juices on my plate after dinner, or for dipping into the litres of gazpacho made in summer – the best soup to quench a thirst.

These small, crunchy, fluffy-on-the-inside rolls might not match the daily bread from the Balearics' 300-year-old bakeries, but it comes pretty close.

1 kg (2 lb 3 oz) stoneground flour, plus extra for dusting
650 ml (22 fl oz) lukewarm water
10 g (⅓ oz) dry active yeast
pinch of granulated sugar
20 g (¾ oz) fine sea salt

Place all the ingredients in the bowl of a stand mixer with the dough hook attached and mix on medium speed for 4–5 minutes, until a rough dough forms.

Transfer the dough to a lightly floured work surface and, using your hands, continue to knead until the dough can be pulled paper-thin without tearing when stretched. Cover with a clean, damp tea towel and set aside to rest for 1½–2 hours in a warm, draught-free spot until risen by one-third.

Place the dough on a well-floured work surface and shape into a thick log. Lightly flour your tea towel, then cover the bread again and set aside for a further 1¼ hours or until risen by another one-third. Divide the dough into four equal portions and shape into rolls about 5 cm (2 in) thick. Cover again with the floured tea towel and set aside to rest for a final 20 minutes.

Preheat the oven to the highest possible temperature (above 230°C/445°F fan-forced). Place a baking tray in the oven to heat up.

Make a deep slash down the centre of each roll and carefully place on the heated tray inside the oven. Bake for 5 minutes, then lower the temperature to 190°C (375°F) and bake for a further 15 minutes or until the bread is golden on top.

Allow to cool completely before serving, so the steam trapped inside continues to cook the bread and crisps up the crust.

Mallorcan rye bread

Bread rolls

COCA D' ALBERCOC

Apricot and potato tart

SERVES 4–6

Throughout summer in Mallorca, you'll find this brioche cake on hotel breakfast buffet menus for the package-tourist hordes, in every 'panaderia' and even topped with sobrassada for an incredible mix of sweet, savoury and umami.

This recipe uses potatoes, which are easier to grow than grains due to the humidity and lack of land space on the islands. Use any seasonal fruit you like – apricots are traditional, but I sometimes mix it up a little. It's even amazing without fruit, as the potato adds a moist density to this traditional and unique cake.

300 g (10½ oz) large potatoes
10 g (⅓ oz) dry active yeast
60 ml (2 fl oz/¼ cup) full-cream (whole) milk, warmed
3 free-range eggs
170 g (6 oz/¾ cup) caster (superfine) sugar
120 g (4½ oz) lard or unsalted butter, softened, plus extra for greasing
2 tablespoons olive oil, plus extra for greasing
1 teaspoon sea salt flakes
400 g (14 oz) baker's flour
8–10 apricots, halved, stones removed
2 tablespoons granulated sugar
icing (confectioners') sugar, for dusting

Place the potatoes in a large saucepan and cover with cold water. Bring to the boil over high heat and cook for 30–35 minutes, until soft but not falling apart. Drain and set aside until cool enough to handle, then peel the skins and push the potato through a ricer or mouli into a large bowl while still warm.

Combine the yeast, warm milk and a teaspoon of the caster sugar in a small jug and set aside to activate.

Whisk the eggs in a large bowl, then whisk in the remaining caster sugar until creamy and pale. Add the lard or butter, oil, warm potato, salt and yeast mixture and mix well to combine. Rain in the flour a little at a time, incorporating it to form a sticky dough. Lightly grease your hands with oil and bring the dough together, kneading in the bowl to form a smooth, elastic ball. Cover with plastic wrap and set aside in a warm place for 1 hour or until risen by one-third.

Preheat the oven to 170°C (340°F) fan-forced. Line a 27 cm (10¾ in) cake tin (or a rectangular 32 x 22 cm/12¾ x 8¾ in tin) with baking paper and grease with a smidge of butter.

Transfer the dough to the tin and smooth the surface. Gently push the apricot halves, cut side down, into the dough, then set aside for a further 30–45 minutes, until risen by another one-third.

Sprinkle the granulated sugar over the top and bake for 30–35 minutes, until golden.

Remove from the oven and allow to cool before dusting the top with icing sugar. Slice and serve.

BUNYOLS DE LES VERGES

Virgin doughnuts

MAKES 20

These potato-based doughnuts mark the story of Saint Ursula and her companions who were murdered by barbarian troops while travelling from Brittany to Rome in the 4th century. Although the exact numbers are unknown, the legend talks about Saint Ursula and the eleven thousand virgins, and in Mallorca the festival of the 'verges' is celebrated on 21 October. On the eve of this festival, local men sing serenades to the women and hand them carnations, then the women reciprocate by giving them these doughnuts. They are delicious with a hot chocolate or simply on their own lathered in sugar or honey.

500 g (1 lb 2 oz) desiree potatoes
7 g (¼ oz) dry active yeast
125 ml (4 fl oz/½ cup) warm water
2 large free-range egg yolks
pinch of sea salt flakes
250 g (9 oz/1⅔ cups) plain (all-purpose) flour
1 litre (34 fl oz/4 cups) vegetable oil, for deep-frying
100 g (3½ oz) granulated sugar

Place the potatoes in a large saucepan and cover with cold water. Bring to the boil over high heat and cook for 30–35 minutes, until soft but not falling apart. Drain and set aside until cool enough to handle, then peel the skins and push the potato through a ricer or mouli into a large bowl while still warm.

In a small bowl or jug, combine the yeast and water and set aside for 5–8 minutes to activate.

Incorporate the egg yolks one by one into the potato, then add the yeast mixture. Stir through the salt, then add the flour in four batches, incorporating each batch before adding the next, until you have a smooth dough-like batter. Cover with a damp tea towel and set aside in a draught-free spot for 1 hour or until risen by one-third.

Heat the oil in a large frying pan or wok to 175°C (345°F) on a kitchen thermometer. Place a bowl of water next to the stovetop to dip your hands in while handling the dough.

With wet hands, tear off 1 tablespoon of dough and, using your thumb, press a small hole through the middle. Carefully drop the dough into the hot oil and fry for 1–2 minutes on each side until golden. Repeat with the remaining dough to make 20 doughnuts.

Drain the doughnuts on a tray lined with paper towel. Transfer to a large bowl, toss in the sugar and eat while still warm.

DOBELGATS

Folded puffs

MAKES 24

Doblegats, meaning 'folded', are sweet little pastry puffs from Mallorca. You'll specifically find them in a village called Manacor served for morning tea with a 'café con leche'.

Choose your favourite filling – chocolate or vanilla custard works well – or use the angel hair pumpkin and apple jam on page 57, as I have done here. Look for a good-quality all-butter puff pastry to achieve a thin, crispy layering.

6 good-quality frozen puff pastry sheets
plain (all-purpose) flour, for dusting
160 g (5½ oz/½ cup) Angel hair pumpkin and apple jam
    (see page 57) or filling of your choice

Preheat the oven to 200°C (400°F) fan-forced. Line a baking tray with baking paper.

Defrost the puff pastry sheets until they're soft but still cold.

Lightly flour a work surface and place a puff pastry sheet on top. Lightly flour the top of the pastry and divide into four even squares. Place 1½ teaspoons of your chosen filling in the centre of each square. Dab the edges with a little water and fold the pastry over, but don't completely seal. Repeat with the remaining pastry and filling.

Transfer the filled pastries to the prepared tray and bake for 20 minutes or until puffed up and golden.

Allow to cool on a wire rack, then serve with strong coffee.

BUNYOLS DE VENT

Ibizan doughnuts

MAKES 20–25

Lent in Ibiza may still exist for some of the locals, but this is the island of vices and when I was there, these doughnuts were the bad habit I was not prepared to give up. They helped me to get up every morning when I knew I had a long, hard day of work ahead of me. I would drag myself across the plaza and over to the bakery in Santa Gertrudis to buy a bag of these soggy alarm clocks. It was a truly religious experience!

This is a very wet batter to work with, but they fry up well and are extremely moist thanks to the potato in the dough. They are also addictive, with a distinct aniseed flavour that keeps you coming back for more, day after day! If you prefer, you can fill them with custard – just fill a piping bag with a small nozzle attached and pierce into the cooked doughnuts once cooled.

1 potato, peeled
150 ml (5 fl oz) full-cream (whole)
   milk, warmed
7 g (¼ oz) dry active yeast
100 ml (3½ fl oz) warm water
200 g (7 oz/1⅓ cups) plain (all-purpose) flour
150 g (5½ oz) granulated sugar
pinch of fine sea salt

1 free-range egg, lightly beaten
100 ml (3½ fl oz) anise liqueur
50 ml (1¾ fl oz) extra virgin olive oil
zest of ¼ orange
2 litres (68 fl oz/8 cups) vegetable oil,
   for deep-frying
1 tablespoon caster (superfine) sugar
2 teaspoons aniseed

Place the potato in a large saucepan and cover with cold water. Bring to the boil over high heat and cook for 20 minutes or until completely soft. Drain and transfer the potato to a large bowl. Add the warm milk and mash together until well combined and no lumps are present. You can also use a hand-held blender for a really smooth purée.

Combine the yeast and water in a small jug and set aside for 5–8 minutes to activate.

In a large bowl or using a stand mixer with the paddle attached, combine the flour, granulated sugar and salt. Incorporate the egg, liqueur, oil, zest and yeast mixture, then add the potato purée and fold through until well combined. Cover, and leave to stand in the bowl for 45–60 minutes until risen by one-third.

Heat the oil in a large heavy-based saucepan to 180°C (350°F) on a kitchen thermometer.

Dip a metal tablespoon into the hot oil, then take a spoonful of batter and lower it into the oil, sliding it off using another spoon. Fry for 2–3 minutes on each side until golden, then set aside on a tray lined with paper towel to drain. Repeat with the remaining batter to make 20–25 doughnuts.

Transfer the doughnuts to a serving bowl and toss through the caster sugar and aniseed while still warm. Serve immediately.

ENSAÏMADAS

Mallorcan spiral pastries

MAKES 9

The name of this famous pastry comes from the Catalan word 'saïm' (pork lard), which stems from the Arabic 'shahim', meaning fat. No one can steal the identity of this international sensation, which can be found as close as mainland Spain and as far away as the Philippines and Latin America. It's the texture that keeps people coming back for more.

The ferry ride from Palma to Barcelona smells of this Mallorcan delight and large, breakfast table-sized versions are neatly tied up in hexagonal boxes for easy transportation by people who really can't live without this local delicacy. You'll need a large oven if you're going to make one big pastry, so I recommend making individual ensaïmadas.

14 g (½ oz) dry active yeast
180 ml (6 fl oz) full-cream (whole) milk, warmed
2 large free-range eggs
1 free-range egg yolk
40 ml (1¼ fl oz) vegetable oil, plus extra
    for greasing
125 g (4½ oz) caster (superfine) sugar

500 g (1 lb 2 oz) baker's flour
pinch of fine sea salt
250 g (9 oz) lard or unsalted butter, softened
630 g (1 lb 6 oz/2 cups) Angel hair pumpkin
    and apple jam (see page 57) (optional)
80 g (2¾ oz) unsalted butter, softened
3 tablespoons icing (confectioners') sugar

Dilute the yeast in a small bowl with the warmed milk and set aside for 5 minutes to activate.

Beat the whole eggs, egg yolk and oil in a large bowl or using a stand mixer with the dough hook attached. Add the diluted yeast mixture and beat or combine on medium–low speed, then add the caster sugar and mix again. Incorporate the flour 150 g (5½ oz/1 cup) at a time, then add the salt and continue to knead until you have a soft, smooth dough.

Grease a work surface with a little oil, tip the dough onto the surface and knead for 5 minutes, folding it onto itself several times to create an elastic and smooth-textured dough. Oil your hands as you go to stop the dough from sticking.

Transfer the dough to a large oiled bowl, cover with plastic wrap and set aside for 1 hour or until risen by one-third. Portion the dough into nine 100 g (3½ oz) pieces.

Oil your work surface again, along with a rolling pin. Working with one piece of dough at a time, roll each piece into a 15 x 60 cm (6 x 24 in) rectangle. With a pastry brush, lather 2 tablespoons of lard over each rectangle of dough. With lightly greased hands, gently stretch the dough lengthways, stretching it a further 10–15 cm (4–6 in) each side without tearing it too much, if possible. If you are making filled ensaïmadas, evenly spoon the jam in a line along one long end of the dough, leaving a 1 cm (½ in) border. Fold the dough over the jam and roll up into a long log. Set aside on a baking tray lined with baking paper and repeat with the remaining dough to create nine logs.

Oil your hands again and gently stretch the logs a little further. Transfer to another baking tray lined with baking paper and curl each log into a spiral, leaving a slight gap between the rows of coils. Tuck the tail ends under the base of each ensaïmada, then cover and set aside in a draught-free spot for 1½ hours or until risen by one-third.

Preheat the oven to 190°C (375°F) fan-forced. Bake the ensaïmadas for 10–12 minutes, until golden brown. Remove from the oven, brush with the softened butter while hot, then transfer to a wire rack to cool.

Once completely cool, finely sift the icing sugar over the ensaïmadas and serve with a hot chocolate or strong coffee.

ENSAÏMA

The exact origins of this unique Balearic Island coiled pastry are not known, but it has appeared at celebratory feasts and religious festivals for as long as anyone can remember. A sweet ambassador for the islands, ensaïmadas travel to the mainland on regular pilgrimages, carried by tourists returning home clutching their precious cargo as hand luggage for gifts to loved ones.

If you're fortunate enough to receive this large, doughy spiral, you may find it filled with traditional pumpkin jam or sobrassada – or a mix of both at Christmas time! Custard, whipped cream, chocolate and local fruit jams, such as apricot, fig and peach, also make regular appearances.

The plain, unfilled and most traditional, however, is the 'ensaïmada lisa', which is usually smaller and heavily sprinkled with icing (confectioners') sugar. This more simple pastry is often eaten daily for morning tea with a strong coffee or hot chocolate to help you through the day.

Never a bite wasted, ensaïmadas taste like a croissant paired with a brioche that's been incubated in lard. If they're not eaten all at once, they will be used the following day in many an inventive up-cycled dessert. They make for an exceptional bread and butter pudding (see page 249) or they can be transformed into a traditional 'turrón' (nougat), where they live on and on.

CÓC PAGÈS DE NADAL

Christmas aniseed bread

MAKES 15 ROLLS OR 2 MEDIUM LOAVES

This sweetened bread is usually accompanied by a rather peculiar 'Christmas sauce'. Very traditional on the Pituïsas (Ibiza and Formentera), the bread is dipped into a blended sweet almond, beef stock, egg and pepper sauce with a few spices and herbs thrown in, including that all-important Balearic Island flavour, aniseed. The bread is mostly made into large loaves, but I like making individual dinner rolls for everyone around the table or serving them for afternoon tea with a good strong coffee, or even alongside a hearty wintery soup.

I have skipped the Christmas sauce in this recipe!

125 ml (4 fl oz/½ cup) full-cream (whole) milk
30 g (1 oz) fresh yeast or 14 g (½ oz) dry
    active yeast
100 g (3½ oz) caster (superfine) sugar
500 g (1 lb 2 oz) baker's flour, plus extra
    for dusting
3 free-range eggs

100 g (3½ oz) lard or softened butter
60 ml (2 fl oz/¼ cup) anise liqueur
zest of ½ lemon
½ teaspoon ground cinnamon
2 teaspoons aniseed
50 g (1¾ oz) icing (confectioners') sugar
    (optional)

Warm the milk in a saucepan to 30–35°C (85–95°F) on a kitchen thermometer. Stir the yeast into the warm milk until completely dissolved, then add 1 teaspoon of the caster sugar.

Place half the flour in a large bowl and make a well in the centre. Pour in the milk mixture and gradually incorporate the flour to form a rough dough. Cover and set aside for 20 minutes or until risen by one-third.

Whisk two of the eggs in a large heatproof bowl or in the bowl of a stand mixer, then whisk in the remaining caster sugar until creamy and pale. Add the lard or butter, liqueur, lemon zest, cinnamon and aniseed. Gradually add the remaining flour, mixing to create a smooth, even dough.

Using your hands or the dough hook attachment of your stand mixer, combine the two doughs to form a smooth, round ball. Cover with a clean, damp tea towel and set aside to rest for 2–3 hours, until risen by one-third.

Line two baking trays with baking paper.

Portion the dough into 15 balls and transfer to the prepared trays. Set aside for 45–60 minutes in a warm, draught-free spot until risen by one-third. Alternatively, halve the dough into two balls and set aside for a further 2–3 hours, until risen by one-third. Shape the dough into long rolls or ciabatta-shaped loaves, transfer to the prepared trays and rest for a final 15 minutes.

Preheat the oven to 150°C (300°F) fan-forced.

Beat the remaining egg and brush the tops of the rolls or loaves. Bake for 1 hour or until golden on top.

Remove from the oven, set aside on a wire rack to cool and serve with the icing sugar dusted over the top, unless serving with soup, in which case serve plain.

MANTEGADES D'AMETLLA

Almond cookies

MAKES 20

You can make these soft and crumbly cookies using butter instead of lard but they won't be the same. They are made by drying out the ingredients and then adding lard, which brings everything together. Commercially, they are then wrapped in tissue paper and twirled at the ends. When it's time to eat, you squeeze the parcel in the palm of your hand and the warmth and heat from your hand melts the lard, so the cookie doesn't crumble everywhere!

200 g (7 oz) blanched almonds
400 g (14 oz) baker's flour, plus extra for dusting
200 g (7 oz) lard
200 g (7 oz) icing (confectioners') sugar, sifted
4 drops of almond extract
2 teaspoons sesame seeds

Preheat the oven to 180°C (350°F) fan-forced.

Place the almonds on a baking tray and bake for 5–7 minutes, until just starting to colour. Allow to cool completely, then blitz in a food processor to a fine powder.

Meanwhile, spread the flour on another baking tray and bake, stirring occasionally, for 6–8 minutes, until lightly toasted. Allow to cool then combine with the ground almonds.

In a stand mixer with the paddle attached, beat the lard until soft and creamy, then beat in the icing sugar and almond extract. Gradually add the toasted flour and almond mixture until you have a crumbly dough.

Divide the dough into two portions, separately wrap in plastic wrap and flatten out into discs. Refrigerate for 20–30 minutes to firm up.

Reduce the oven temperature to 170°C (340°F). Line two baking trays with baking paper.

Working with one piece of dough at a time, roll the dough out on a floured work surface to an even 2 cm (¾ in) thickness. Using a 4 cm (1½ in) cookie cutter, cut out 20 rounds and place on the prepared trays.

Sprinkle the sesame seeds over the top of each cookie, then bake for 20–22 minutes, until lightly golden. Transfer to a wire rack to cool.

The cookies will keep in an airtight container in the pantry for up to 1 week.

CRESPELLS MENORQUIN

Menorcan jam drops

MAKES 12

Jewish in origin, these thick, unleavened cookies were traditionally shaped like the Star of David. On Mallorca, they make them into hearts, flowers and even animals, while on Menorca they're filled with homemade jams, sobrassada (of course) or sweet potato. Whichever shape you decide on, you'll need two cookie cutter sizes to make the jam drop centre visible.

450 g (1 lb/3 cups) plain (all-purpose) flour, plus extra for dusting
100 g (3½ oz) icing (confectioners') sugar, plus extra for dusting
200 g (7 oz) lard or butter, diced
2 free-range egg yolks
80 ml (2½ fl oz/⅓ cup) full-cream (whole) milk
300 g (10½ oz) apricot jam or jam of your choice (see Note)

Preheat the oven to 180°C (350°F) fan-forced. Line two baking trays with baking paper.

In a large bowl, combine the flour and sugar. Mix the lard or butter through with your fingertips to form large breadcrumbs. Add the egg yolks and mix to combine, then add the milk, one teaspoon at a time, until you have a smooth, combined dough.

Transfer the dough to a floured work surface and knead for 5 minutes or until you have a smooth and elastic dough. Wrap the dough in plastic wrap and refrigerate for 20–30 minutes to firm up.

Transfer the dough to a floured work surface and roll out to a 4 mm (¼ in) thickness. Using a 6.5 cm (2½ in) cookie cutter, cut out 24 circles of dough, re-rolling the dough offcuts as you go. Using a 2.5 cm (1 in) cookie cutter, cut out the centre of half the dough circles.

Place the circles on the prepared trays and add 1 teaspoon of filling to the centre of each cookie base. Top with the cut-out dough circles, so the jam is poking through the middle.

Bake for 10 minutes or until golden around the edges. Transfer to a wire rack to cool before dusting with icing sugar.

NOTE: Make sure the jam you use is quite thick, so it doesn't melt too much and spill out of the cookies.

Almond cookies

Biscuit ears

Menorcan jam
drops

ORELLANES

Cookie ears

MAKES 20–24

Meaning 'big ears', 'orellenes' is also the name given to dried apricots in Catalan. These cookies are traditionally found in Artà, Mallorca, where some villages perfume these crispy little addictions with anise liqueur or orange zest. You'll also find a version of 'orellenes' over in Ibiza where they are actually shaped like ears and made with a fluffy, doughnut-style dough.

1 tablespoon freshly squeezed lemon juice
150 ml (5 fl oz) full-cream (whole) milk
100 g (3½ oz) lard, at room temperature
1 free-range egg
400 g (14 oz) baker's flour, plus extra for dusting
1 litre (34 fl oz/4 cups) vegetable oil, for deep-frying
icing (confectioners') sugar, for dusting

Whisk the lemon juice, milk, lard and egg in a large bowl. Gradually add the flour and incorporate it into the mixture using a wooden spoon or your fingertips, until the ingredients come together to form a smooth dough. Set aside to rest for 10 minutes.

Roll the dough out on a floured work surface until it is about 3 mm (⅛ in) thick, dusting the top with flour as you roll to prevent it from sticking. Cut the dough into uneven rectangular shapes, about 3 x 5 cm (1¼ x 2 in).

Heat the oil in a large frying pan to 180°C (350°F) on a kitchen thermometer. Working in batches, fry the dough until puffed up and golden, then transfer to paper towel to absorb any excess oil.

Allow the 'orellenes' to cool, then generously sift over some icing sugar. Serve on a large platter and enjoy straight away.

ROBIOLS

Ricotta and quince turnovers

MAKES 10–15

Many traditional dishes start in the family home, passed down through the generations. This is one of those recipes that unites everyone – made in a large batch by the whole family in a party atmosphere, and then shared among everyone at the end.

These turnovers are typically made with pumpkin jam and eaten at Christmas and Easter, but I love using ricotta and quince paste, especially at Christmas, to make a change from the regular cheese board.

100 g (3½ oz) lard or butter, at room temperature
2 tablespoons extra virgin olive oil
3 tablespoons freshly squeezed orange juice
2 tablespoons sweet white wine
1 free-range egg yolk
100 g (3½ oz) caster (superfine) sugar
500 g (1 lb 2 oz) plain (all-purpose) flour, plus extra for dusting

Ricotta and quince filling
200 g (7 oz) good-quality firm ricotta
2 tablespoons caster (superfine) sugar
50 g (1¾ oz) quince paste, cut into small dice

Place the lard or butter and olive oil in the bowl of a stand mixer with the whisk attached and beat until combined. Add the orange juice, wine, egg yolk and sugar and mix on medium speed for a few minutes to form a paste.

Swap the whisk for the dough hook attachment, add the flour and knead for 4–5 minutes on medium speed until a dough forms. Cut the dough in half, wrap both halves tightly in plastic wrap and refrigerate for 15–20 minutes.

Meanwhile, to make the filling, combine the ricotta and sugar in a bowl and set aside.

Preheat the oven to 170°C (340°F) fan-forced. Line two baking trays with baking paper.

Working with one half of dough at a time, transfer the dough to a floured work surface and roll it out as thinly as possible.

Using a round 10 cm (4 in) cookie cutter, cut out as many circles as possible, re-rolling any dough offcuts, until it's all used up.

Place 1 tablespoon of the ricotta filling on one half of each dough circle, leaving a 1–1.5 cm (½ in) border and press a few cubes of quince paste into the filling.

Brush a little water around the edges, then fold over the unfilled half of dough and seal, using a fork to crimp the edges. Place on the prepared trays and bake for 20–25 minutes, until golden and cooked through (see note).

NOTE: Lard doesn't burn as fast as butter so if substituting butter, watch the oven time as the turnovers will colour a lot faster.

PANADES

Lamb pies

MAKES 8

Every country has a favourite pie and Spain is no exception. Distinguished by its filling and shape, these curious Balearic-style empanadas (meaning to wrap up) are individually 'sculpted' like clay, then filled and 'fired' in the oven. Although an unusual addition, the orange juice in the dough softens the richness of the lard.

100 g (3½ oz) lard or butter, at room temperature
60 ml (2 fl oz/¼ cup) extra virgin olive oil, plus extra for greasing
180 ml (6 fl oz) freshly squeezed orange juice
pinch of fine sea salt
500 g (1 lb 2 oz) plain (all-purpose) flour, plus extra for dusting

Lamb filling
400 g (14 oz) boneless lamb shoulder, cut into 2 cm (¾ in) dice
120 g (4½ oz) sobrassada (see page 216)
120 g (4½ oz) pancetta, diced
1½ teaspoons smoked pimentòn
1½ tablespoons extra-virgin olive oil
200 g (7 oz) frozen peas
sea salt flakes and freshly ground black pepper

Place the lard or butter and oil in the bowl of a stand mixer with the whisk attached and beat until combined. Add the orange juice and fine sea salt and mix on medium speed for a few minutes to form a paste.

Swap the whisk for the dough hook attachment, add the flour and knead for 4–5 minutes on medium speed until a dough forms. Wrap tightly in plastic wrap and refrigerate for 15–20 minutes.

Meanwhile combine the filling ingredients, except the peas, in a bowl and season with salt and pepper. Set aside.

Preheat the oven to 160°C (320°F) fan-forced. Line two baking trays with baking paper.

Transfer the dough to a floured work surface and roll into a large log. Portion the dough into eight 55 g (2 oz) pieces (save the remaining dough for the pie lids). Working with one piece of dough at a time, roll the dough into a circle and use it to line the base and side of a small bowl with a 5 cm (2 in) base. Grease your fingers with a little oil if the dough is starting to stick. Carefully remove the moulded dough from the bowl and set aside on one of the prepared trays. Refrigerate while you prepare the pie lids.

Weigh out the remaining dough into eight 20 g (¾ oz) balls and roll each ball into a 6.5 cm (2½ in) circle.

Divide the filling evenly among the pie bases, leaving a 1–1.5 cm (½ in) gap at the top. Sprinkle the peas over the top and brush a little water around the edges. Drape the lids over the pie bases and pinch the dough together to form a seal.

Bake for 40–45 minutes, until golden and cooked through.

Set the pies aside on a wire rack to cool slightly and to allow the filling to continue cooking before serving.

Enjoy warm or at room temperature.

BAKERY

COCARROIS

Vegetable pasties

MAKES 18

Originally from the Levant, these vegetarian savoury pasties are popular picnic fare throughout the Balearics. They're made with any combination of local seasonal vegetables, but they always include pine nuts and raisins, which are abundant throughout the region.

100 g (3½ oz) lard or butter, at room temperature
60 ml (2 fl oz/¼ cup) extra virgin olive oil, plus extra for greasing
180 ml (6 fl oz) freshly squeezed orange juice
pinch of fine sea salt
500 g (1 lb 2 oz) plain (all-purpose) flour, plus extra for dusting

Vegetable filling
300 g (10½ oz) silverbeet (Swiss chard), stalks removed, leaves finely chopped
200 g (7 oz) cauliflower florets, finely chopped
2 marinated artichoke hearts, finely chopped
1 tablespoon extra virgin olive oil
½ bunch chives, finely chopped
2 tablespoons pine nuts
2 tablespoons raisins
½ teaspoon ground cinnamon
sea salt flakes and freshly ground black pepper

Place the lard or butter and oil in the bowl of a stand mixer with the whisk attached and beat until combined. Add the orange juice and salt and mix on medium speed for a few minutes to form a paste.

Swap the whisk for the dough hook attachment, add the flour and knead for 4–5 minutes on medium speed until a dough forms. Wrap tightly in plastic wrap and refrigerate for 15–20 minutes.

Meanwhile, combine the filling ingredients in a bowl and set aside.

Preheat the oven to 170°C (340°F) fan-forced. Line two baking trays with baking paper.

Transfer the dough to a floured work surface and roll into a large log. Portion the dough into eighteen 75 g (2¾ oz) pieces and roll each one into a ball. Flatten the balls with the palms of your hands (grease your hands with a little oil if the dough is starting to stick) or use a rolling pin to create 12 cm (4¾ in) circles.

Set aside on the prepared trays and place in the fridge for 10 minutes to firm up slightly.

Spoon 1 tablespoon of the filling in a thick line along the left side of one dough circle. Brush the edge with a little water and fold the right side of dough over the filling. Pinch the dough all the way around to form a seal. Repeat with the remaining dough and filling.

Bake for 40–45 minutes, until golden and cooked through.

Set the pasties aside on a wire rack to cool slightly and to allow the filling to continue cooking before serving.

Eat warm or at room temperature on a hot day.

Lamb pies

Vegetable pasties

LANA

aking the most of surplus produce through conserving techniques, such as pickling, fermenting, brining, freezing, drying, canning, smoking and salting, dates back thousands of years. Traditionally a largely agrarian society, the need to store provisions for leaner times, transport and trade was paramount to life on the Balearics, and many of the recipes and techniques employed have stood the test of time. This long-lasting tradition of making food at home transformed raw, often indigestible staples, such as olives, capers and other indigenous plants on the islands into edible, surplus produce, which could be paired with fresh food throughout the year.

At harvest time, excess crops of overripe fruit were turned into homemade jams, pastes, condiments and spreads, or dried to use in breads and cakes. The famous 'cabell d'àngel' jam (see page 57) is made with siam pumpkin, a gourd vine grown throughout Mallorca where it thrives in dry and humid conditions. Although a vegetable, this unusual ingredient must be cooked with sugar to be really enjoyed, and it is most famously used as a filling for the classic ensaïmada (see page 32).

In addition to conserving food, homebrew alcohol has long been a favourite pastime for many islanders, with local families keeping their best-loved moonshine recipes a closely guarded secret. From homemade red wine left to age in the garage to the much-loved 'herbes' (herb liqueur, see page 82) – a distilled concoction of local herbs and anise liqueur often served at the end of the evening meal – there is always something to share with the neighbourhood during celebrations.

Today, local charcuterie, such as, camaïot, botifarron, carnixulla and cuixot from Menorca, along with the islands' most famous export, sobrassada (see page 216), are readily available throughout the year thanks to the advent of commerical curing techniques. Fish and seafood products are usually brined and pickled with local herbs and spices for their long-lasting properties, and then tinned or bottled for longterm storage.

If you like to preserve your own surplus produce or even if you're just curious about the process and culture behind some of the Balearics' most tried and tested 'casolana' (homemade) recipes, then this chapter provides some unique and traditional techniques to make the most of any seasonal abundance you may have at your disposal.

MELMELADA DE LLIMONA

Lemon marmalade

MAKES ENOUGH TO FILL 1 x 600 ML (20½ FL OZ) JAR

Marmalade was said to have been invented when a cargo of oranges washed up on the shores of Dundee, Scotland, after a Spanish ship ran aground during the British occupation of Menorca. You will find many British influences in the pastry shops on the island, from the humble sponge to meringues and lemon tart. Of course, lemons are a huge part of Mediterranean cuisine. We know they always accompany fish and they're even served in finger bowls to clean your hands, but marrying them with sugar? What a great way to enjoy their bitterness and acidity.

This lemon marmalade is a perfect spread or filling for any number of pastries you might indulge in. Serve it with freshly baked croissants, ensaïmadas or just simply with butter on toast.

1 kg (2 lb 3 oz) lemons
800 g (1 lb 12 oz) caster (superfine) sugar
pinch of sea salt flakes
1 cinnamon stick
3 thyme sprigs

Clean the lemons, then place in a large saucepan, cover with water and bring to the boil. Reduce the heat to a simmer and cook for 45–60 minutes, until the lemons are soft when pierced with a knife. Drain and set aside to cool.

Slice the ends off the lemons and discard. Quarter the lemons and scoop out the flesh and seeds into a fine sieve set over a saucepan to act as a drip bowl underneath. Squash the flesh through the strainer into the saucepan, then place the remaining pulp and pips in a square of muslin (cheesecloth) and tie with kitchen string. Place in the saucepan with the lemon juice and flesh.

Remove any remaining white pith from the rind and cut the rind into even-sized strips as thick or as thin as you would like. Add the rind to the saucepan, along with the remaining ingredients and 250 ml (8½ fl oz/1 cup) of water. Bring to a rolling boil and stir until the sugar has dissolved, then reduce to a simmer and cook for 20–30 minutes. The longer you cook the mixture, the stringier and darker the marmalade will be.

Remove and discard the cinnamon, then spoon the jam into a sterilised 600 ml (20½ fl oz) glass jar (see Note) while hot, then tightly seal and turn upside-down to cool. Once cool, put the jar through the dishwasher to clean and reinforce the heat seal.

The marmalade will keep in a cool, dry spot for 4–6 months.

NOTE: To sterilise glass jars, wash the jars and lids in hot, soapy water and remove any labels or residual food. Preheat the oven to 110°C (230°F) fan-forced, place the jars and lids upside down on clean wire racks and place in the oven for 10–12 minutes, until dry. Transfer to a clean tea towel, right side up, and fill as directed.

CABELL D'ÀNGEL I POMA

Angel hair pumpkin and apple jam

MAKES ENOUGH TO FILL 2 x 500 ML (17 FL OZ) JARS

Angel hair jam from Mallorca is a popular filling for pastries across the Balearic Islands and throughout mainland Spain. It's made using the fibrous flesh of the siam pumpkin, which can be hard to get hold of, so here I've used spaghetti squash, which gives a similar stringy, thread-like result, only in a deep amber colour rather than the original clear, transparent sweet jam of the islands.

1 spaghetti squash, cut in half lengthways, seeds removed
3 red apples, peeled, roughly chopped
450 g (1 lb) caster (superfine) sugar
juice of 1 lemon
zest of ½ lemon

Preheat the oven to 200°C (400°F) fan-forced. Line a baking tray with baking paper.

Place the squash, flesh side down, on the prepared tray and bake for 30 minutes or until the skin starts to soften.

Allow to cool slightly, then scoop out the flesh into a saucepan – you should have about 1 kg (2 lb 3 oz). Add the apple, sugar, lemon juice and zest and gently cook over medium-low heat, stirring regularly, for 20–25 minutes, until the sugar has dissolved and the mixture has thickened.

If you are going to use the jam within a few days, set aside in a bowl to cool, then keep covered in the fridge. Alternatively, transfer to two 500 ml (17 fl oz) sterilised jars (see Note opposite) while the jam is still hot, tightly seal and turn upside-down to cool. Once cool, put the jars through the dishwasher to clean and reinforce the seals.

The jam will keep in a cool, dry spot for 4–6 months.

HOMEMADE

Angel hair pumpkin and apple jam

Lemon marmalade

CONFITURA DE TOMÀTIGA

Tomato jam

MAKES ENOUGH TO FILL 3 x 350 ML (12½ OZ) JARS

The 'tomatiga de ramallet' is a Mallorcan variety of tomato that you'll find growing from vines hanging over old stone walls or spread across the ground, where there's a lot of radiated heat. They're the last of the summer crop, picked when they're still orangey green and strung up and left to mature to use over the winter months. The thick pulp has fewer seeds, making them perfect for rubbing on stale bread for the famous 'pa amb tomàquet' (bread with tomato) or for turning into jam. Here, I've used late-summer ripe roma (plum) tomatoes, which make a perfectly good substitute.

2 kg (4 lb 6 oz) ripe roma (plum) tomatoes
400 g (14 oz) caster (superfine) sugar
300 g (10½ oz) brown sugar
1 lemon
1 star anise
1 teaspoon sea salt flakes
½ teaspoon freshly ground black pepper

Using a sharp knife, score a cross in the base of the tomatoes. Bring a saucepan of water to the boil and blanch the tomatoes for 2 minutes or until the skins start to curl away from the flesh. Immediately drain and plunge into iced water and peel away the skins. Cut the tomatoes in half crossways and scoop out the seeds. Chop the flesh into small, even dice and place in a large bowl with the sugars. Mix well and set aside for 10–15 minutes, until the tomato juice leaches out.

Zest half the lemon and add to the chopped tomato. Squeeze the juice into a small bowl, then place the remaining pulp and pips in a square of muslin (cheesecloth) and tie with kitchen string.

Place the tomato mixture in a large stockpot with the muslin bag, star anise, salt and pepper and bring to the boil over high heat. Boil for 35–40 minutes, then reduce the heat and gently simmer for a further 40 minutes or until most of the liquid has evaporated. Remove from the heat and stir through the lemon juice.

Spoon the tomato jam into three 350 ml (12½ fl oz) sterilised glass jars (see Note on page 56) while still hot, then tightly seal and set aside upside-down to cool. Once cool, put the jars through the dishwasher to clean and reinforce the heat seal.

The jam will keep in a cool, dry spot for 4–6 months.

PA DE FIGA

'Fig bread' paste

MAKES 10

Directly translated as 'fig bread', along with the Italian version 'panaforte' (meaning strong bread), this is actually more of a slice, as traditionally the only flour used was to dust the mould to prevent the fig mixture from sticking. Local villagers would come together at harvest time to make large quantities of this paste as a way to preserve the surplus fruit for winter. Everyone would get involved, from hand-picking and drying the figs to cracking the nuts, collecting the honey, making the straw moulds and then filling and pressing them. I love the thought of sitting around and making food all day with so many helpers!

This recipe makes such a beautiful gift, especially at Christmas time when it's traditionally eaten. It has a good shelf life and is often served as a dessert or digestif with a slice of sharp, bitey cheese, perfect for when you need a little pick-me-up after a large feast.

10 fig leaves
100 g (3½ oz) walnuts
1 teaspoon aniseed
2 teaspoons sesame seeds
750 g (1 lb 11 oz) dried figs
1 tablespoon honey
3 tablespoons anise liqueur or brandy
zest of ½ orange
1 teaspoon finely chopped rosemary leaves
¼ teaspoon freshly ground black pepper
pinch of sea salt flakes
1 tablespoon plain (all-purpose) flour

Blanch the fig leaves in salted boiling water for 30 seconds, then refresh in iced water. Drain and pat dry between two clean tea towels.

In a dry frying pan over medium heat, lightly toast the walnuts, then remove from the pan and set aside. Toast the aniseed and set aside, followed by the sesame seeds. Roughly chop the walnuts and bruise the aniseed using a mortar and pestle. Place the nuts and seeds in a large bowl.

Thinly slice half the figs and toss through the seeds and nuts.

Place the remaining figs, honey, liqueur, orange zest, rosemary, black pepper and salt in the bowl of a food processor and blitz to a paste. Add to the bowl with the sliced figs.

Dust 10 ramekins or large muffin moulds with the flour, then line with the fig leaves, vein side up, so they hang over the sides. Using wet hands, divide the fig paste among the moulds and press down to evenly flatten. Lift the fig packages out of their moulds and tie up with kitchen string to secure. You can hang them up by the string or leave them on a wire rack in a cool, dry place for 2–3 days before serving.

The fig paste will keep in an airtight container in the fridge for 2–3 months.

Fig 'bread' paste

Pickled rhubarb

Tomato jam

RUIBARBRE

Pickled rhubarb

MAKES ENOUGH TO FILL 1 x 1 LITRE (34 FL OZ) JAR

Another ingredient attributed to the British influence on Menorca, rhubarb is predominately used as a fruit for compotes, jams and jellies or stewed and paired with apple in cakes, crumbles and tarts. Rhubarb is also widely used in Germanic countries and you'll find it on Mallorca where there's a large population of German residents working and living away from their colder roots.

Pickled rhubarb is an excellent way to use up those abundant stalks. They give the best burst of flavour when thinly sliced and mixed through salads, or served with fresh bread and a big wedge of cheese.

400–500 g (14 oz–1 lb 2 oz) rhubarb stalks
300 ml (10 fl oz) apple cider vinegar, plus extra if needed
1 teaspoon fine sea salt
300 g (10½ oz) granulated sugar
1 tablespoon fennel seeds
2 teaspoons black peppercorns

Trim the leaves and base off the rhubarb stalks and cut into lengths a little shorter than the height of your sterilised jar (see Note on page 56). Arrange the stalks so they're standing up inside the jar, but not too tightly packed to allow the pickling liquid to surround the stalks.

Place the vinegar, salt, sugar, fennel seeds, peppercorns and 300 ml (10 fl oz) of water in a saucepan and bring to a rolling boil. Remove from the heat and pour over the rhubarb, filling the jar to the rim. Add a little more vinegar to get you there if you don't quite make it.

Set aside to cool completely, then tightly seal with the lid and set aside in a cool, dry spot for a minimum of 1 week.

Once opened, the pickled rhubarb will keep in the fridge for up to 6 months.

TÀPERES

Pickled capers

In Menorca, the edible early flower buds of the caper bush are smaller and denser than the big, juicy pods found on commercial shelves, which have been left on the bush for a plumper, more floral result. They can be tricky to grow, but the salt-tolerant and drought-loving nature of this plant makes the Balearics, along with neighbouring Sicily and Pantelleria where the capers are mostly preserved in salt instead of brine, a prime habitat.

Notoriously difficult to harvest because of their thorns, capers are handpicked before flowering. Left on the bush, they will flower and fruit (this is the caper berry). The leaves are also picked and pickled for use in salads, such as the local Mahón potato salad (see page 125) or used as a herb in steak tartare.

Failing access to a flourishing caper bush, I've used nasturtium pods or 'poor man's capers', as they have a similar flavour to the tangy caper with its mustardy notes, but with a little more bitterness and a little less fruit.

500 g (1 lb 2 oz) nasturtium, capers or caper berry pods
50 g (1¾ oz) fine sea salt
250 ml (8½ fl oz/1 cup) white wine vinegar, plus extra if needed
pinch of granulated sugar
¼ lemon, halved

Wash the pods well to remove any dirt, then place in a large non-reactive bowl or bucket and completely cover with water. Place a plate or plastic bag over the surface of the water to stop any air getting in and to keep the pods submerged. Set aside in the fridge for 12 hours, then change the water and chill for another 12 hours.

Dissolve the salt in 300 ml (10 fl oz) of water, then stir through the vinegar.

Strain the pods and spoon into a sterilised 1 litre (34 fl oz) glass jar (see Note on page 56) or use two 500 ml (17 fl oz) glass jars, if you prefer. Slide the lemon down one side of the jar and pour in the brining liquid to the top of the rim. Add a little more vinegar to get you there if you don't quite make it.

Tightly close the lid and set aside in a cool, dry spot for at least 1 week before opening. Once opened, the capers will keep in the fridge for up to 6 months.

HOMEMADE

Pickled nasturtium pods

Pickled sea fennel

Pickled capers

FONOLL MARI

Pickled sea fennel

MAKES ENOUGH TO FILL 1 x 1 LITRE (34 FL OZ) JAR

Sea fennel (rock samphire) is found in abundance all over the Balearic Islands and further afield on many a Mediterranean coastal cliff and even as far as Dover in England. Reminiscent of fennel, it is related to the celery and parsley family. It's high in vitamin C, along with other antioxidant properties, which made it a staple in every pirate's medicine cabinet to avoid nasty cases of scurvy on long pillaging trips.

I used to forage daily for sea fennel on the rocks of S'Estanyol in Ibiza for Karen Martini's restaurant Cala Bonita, where we would serve it quickly blanched alongside chargrilled calamari, a black garlic emulsion, shaved macadamia nuts and fresh lime. Over in Mallorca, pickled sea fennel is served alongside their traditional 'pa amb oli' (bread and oil) (see page 99).

Try growing this plant if you live in a warm, dry climate. As well as being delicious, it's salt tolerant, has gorgeous flowers and keeps producing all year round.

200–250 g (7–9 oz) sea fennel (rock samphire)
2 heaped teaspoons fine sea salt
650 ml (22 fl oz) white wine vinegar

Wash the sea fennel under cold running water to remove any dirt. Trim and discard any thick stalks, then push the fennel into a 1 litre (34 fl oz) sterilised glass jar (see Note on page 56) or use two 500 ml (17 fl oz) jars, if you prefer.

Dissolve the salt in the vinegar and pour over the sea fennel. Fill the jar to the rim with water, then tightly seal with the lid and set aside in a cool, dark spot for a minimum of 4 weeks or until the sea fennel has darkened to the colour of overcooked asparagus.

Serve the pickled sea fennel in salads, with a hard cheese and some quince paste or alongside pan-fried fish in a rich butter sauce.

Once opened, the sea fennel will keep in the fridge for 4–6 months.

HOMEMADE

OLIVES MORTES

Dead olives

MAKES ENOUGH TO FILL 2 x 500 ML (17 FL OZ) JARS

On the Balearic Islands, the slightly sundried and shrivelled olives remaining on the tree after harvest are picked and salt-cured to 'die' a slow, delectable death buried deep in salt. In drought-prone areas, this is a great and traditional way to prepare olives without using any water. The faster, more modern and commercial way is to pick the fruit ripe and freeze it for a few days to 'kill' the olives and then cover them with salt. Another method, and the one I prefer to use as I never have enough room in my freezer, is to boil them before salting. This is also a great way to impart flavour and sterilise them of any bird droppings.

The result is an olive with a shrivelled, wrinkly skin and a really juicy flesh that's salty and slightly bitter in flavour. These olives are great added to pasta sauces and braises, paired with tomatoes in salads or served on their own dressed with fresh herbs, cumin, chilli flakes and lemon zest.

You can halve this recipe, but if you're going to invest in this process I suggest going bulk and even doubling it.

1 kg (2 lb 3 oz) raw black olives
2 tablespoons fine sea salt
2 fresh bay leaves
3 thyme sprigs
500 g (1 lb 2 oz) coarse sea salt (you can use rock salt,
    but it will take another 4–5 days of curing)
2 tablespoons extra virgin olive oil

Puncture each olive a few times with a metal skewer or fork. You may want to wear gloves to protect your skin from the leaching dye.

Fill a large stockpot with 3 litres (3 qts) of water and place over high heat. Add the fine sea salt, bay leaves and thyme and bring to the boil. Add the olives, then remove from the heat and set aside for 5 minutes. Drain off the liquid and spread the olives out on wire racks to air-dry for a few hours. You can also use a blow-dryer to speed things up a little.

In a large bucket or non-reactive mixing bowl, toss the olives with one-third of the coarse salt to evenly coat them. Place another third of salt in the bottom of a large ham bag or old, clean pillowcase and spoon the olives into the bag. Pack the remaining salt on top, then string up the bag over an empty bucket in a cool, dry place and leave to drain and cure.

After 14 days, take an olive, rinse well and taste it. If the olive tastes very bitter, leave them to hang for another week or fortnight. If it's well shrivelled and mild in flavour, remove the olives from the bag and shake off as much salt as you can (you want to avoid rinsing them and rehydrating them with any water). Use a thick pastry brush to remove any residual salt rocks from the olives and lay them out flat again on wire racks overnight to air-dry.

Toss the olives in the olive oil, then divide between two sterilised 500 ml (17 fl oz) glass jars (see Note on page 56) and place in the fridge, where they will keep for 4–6 months.

OLIVES TRENCADES DE L'AVI

Grandma's smashed olives

MAKES ENOUGH TO FILL 2 x 2 LITRE (2 QT) JARS

Perhaps this dish gets its name from the olives that were always on offer at Grandma's house, left over from what didn't make it to the press. They can also look like Grandma sat on your batch of olives and squashed them! This rough smashing of the flesh allows the aromats to penetrate the olives faster, while at the same time releasing more oils and juice to make a cloudy marinade that's very distinct.

Originally made straight from the tree to accelerate the de-bittering process, if you have the time, space and patience to cure the olives yourself it's completely worth it. But don't miss out because you're not set up; just go and buy some good-quality ready-to-eat whole green olives – preferably manzanilla or some local green guys you know about – and start smashing!

2 kg (4 lb 6 oz) raw green olives or good-quality store-bought green olives
350 g (12½ oz) fine sea salt
400 ml (14 fl oz) white wine vinegar
4 fennel flower heads with stalks, chopped
2 long green chillies, chopped
2 lemon leaves
2 garlic cloves
12 white peppercorns
extra virgin olive oil, for drizzling

Wash your olives well under cold running water to remove any debris or dust.

Place the olives in a large bucket and cover with water. Weigh down the olives with a plate or similar to ensure they stay submerged. Change the water daily for 5 days (this will reduce the bitterness and remove a lot of the astringency). You can skip this process if you're using already-brined store-bought olives.

Bring 4 litres (4 qts) of water, the salt and vinegar to a rolling boil and boil for 2 minutes or until the salt is dissolved. Remove from the heat and stir through the fennel, chilli, lemon leaves, garlic and peppercorns. Set aside to cool.

Using a rock, the base of a glass jar or a metal weight, smash open each olive on a sturdy wooden chopping board in one hit. Spoon into two 2 litre (2 qt) sterilised glass jars (see Note on page 56).

Once the brine is completely cool, pour the liquid and aromats into the jars, filling to the rim to avoid any air pockets. Screw the lids on firmly and set aside on a shelf for 2–3 months (or 2–3 weeks if using already-brined olives) in a cool, dry place. Taste-test for bitterness every now and then, but depending on the variety and your personal taste preference they will probably take 4–5 months to cure.

To serve, remove the olives from the brine and drizzle with a little olive oil and some of the aromats from the jar.

Grandma's smashed olives

Dead olives

MUSCLERES EN ESCABETX

Pickled mussels

MAKES ENOUGH TO FILL 1 x 800 ML (27 FL OZ) JAR

Pickled mussels are a Galician tapas hero that have made their way to the Balearics. You can buy very good-quality mussels in tins and jars in Spain, but it's well worth making your own, especially if you have access to local mussels.

Having these on hand in the fridge means I've always got something delicious to eat when I fancy a quick makeshift graze. Eat them cold with a toothpick before dinner or serve them warm alongside a grilled (broiled) piece of fish and some blanched green beans to transform a simple supper.

125 ml (4 fl oz/½ cup) dry white wine
2 fresh bay leaves
1.5 kg (3 lb 5 oz) mussels, scrubbed
1 white onion, thinly sliced
2 Dutch carrots, thinly sliced
1 garlic clove, thinly sliced
150 ml (5 fl oz) sherry vinegar
1 thyme sprig
1 teaspoon sea salt
1 teaspoon granulated sugar
½ teaspoon smoked pimentòn
extra virgin olive oil, for drizzling
chopped parsley leaves, to serve (optional)
crusty bread, to serve

Heat the wine, bay leaves and 125 ml (4 fl oz/½ cup) of water in a large saucepan over high heat. Add the mussels and cook, covered, for 4–6 minutes, until the shells just begin to open. Immediately remove the mussels from the pan and set aside. Leave any unopened stragglers in the pan a little longer to see if they'll open. If they don't, remove and discard. Keep the pan juices simmering until reduced to about 125 ml (4 fl oz/½ cup) of liquid. Strain into a small bowl and set aside.

Once the mussels are cool enough to handle, separate them from the shells, snip out the beards with a pair of scissors and place the mussels in a non-reactive bowl with the onion, carrot and garlic.

Combine the sherry vinegar, thyme, salt, sugar, pimentòn and reserved mussel juice in a non-reactive bowl and set aside to completely cool.

Pour the pickling liquid over the mussels and refrigerate for 4–6 hours or overnight.

To serve, drizzle the pickled mussels with a little oil and scatter over some chopped parsley leaves, if you like. Enjoy with crusty bread for mopping up the juices.

Any left-over mussels will keep in the fridge for 10–14 days if completely submerged in the pickling liquid.

SEITONS

White anchovies

MAKES 500 G (1 LB 2 OZ)

Fondly known in Spanish as 'boquerones', a plate of white anchovies is the ultimate Mediterranean aperitivo, especially served with a beer and some olives. The anchovies are 'cooked' without heat using a popular curing method, which is basically a simple cold pickle made with white vinegar to keep the flesh white.

Make your own from any small local bait fish you can find. I've used garfish in this recipe, which has a delicate, sweet taste.

500 g (1 lb 2 oz) whole garfish or anchovies
fine sea salt
100 ml (3½ fl oz) white wine vinegar, plus extra if needed
200 ml (7 fl oz) white vinegar, plus extra if needed
200 ml (7 fl oz) extra virgin olive oil
4 garlic cloves, thinly sliced
1 teaspoon black and white peppercorns, plus freshly ground black pepper
4 bichos (small dried red chillies) or 1 dried chilli, crumbled (optional)
potato chips (crisps) or olives, to serve

Using a small paring knife, remove the heads from the fish. Make a slit along the belly of each fish and open out flat. Slide the tip of your knife under the spine at the neck and gently pull away the spine, taking the innards with you. I like to leave the tails on to handle them without damaging the flesh too much.

Place the fish in a non-reactive shallow dish, cover with cold water to completely submerge the fillets and add 1 teaspoon of salt. Set aside for 5 minutes, then replace with clean water. Set aside for a further 2 minutes, then rinse and pat each fish dry with paper towel. Clean and dry the dish.

Combine the vinegars in a jug, then pour 150 ml (5 fl oz) into the clean dish, along with 100 ml (3½ fl oz) of water. Lay the fish in the dish, skin side down, then cover with the remaining vinegar. Depending on the size of your dish you may need to add more liquid, in which case always use a ratio of 100 ml (3½ fl oz) of water to 300 ml (10 fl oz) of vinegar, otherwise the fish will over-cure and end up tough and hard. Refrigerate for at least 6 hours but no more than 8 hours.

Remove the fillets from the pickle liquid and place a single layer in another shallow dish. Drizzle with a little of the olive oil, then scatter over a few garlic slices and peppercorns, along with a little chilli (if using). Repeat with the remaining ingredients, finishing with a final layer of oil to cover the fish. Set aside in the fridge to marinate for at least 24 hours, until the flesh has turned white.

Serve the fish with freshly ground black pepper sprinkled over the top and good-quality potato chips or olives on the side.

Any leftover fish will keep covered in the fridge for 12–14 days, if completely submerged in the pickling liquid.

White anchovies

Pickled mussels

GUATLLES EN ESCABETX

Pickled quail

SERVES 4

Before refrigeration, the Spanish preserved meat, fish and vegetables in vinegar (a la 'escabechada'). To prevent spoilage, a strong acidic solution was used, but over time the recipe evolved and now the concentration of vinegar is much lighter, enabling it to also be served as a dressing.

The maceration of these inexpensive and now mainly farmed birds aids tenderisation and mellows out the flavour a little. Pickled quail are great to have hanging around the fridge and they will liven up many a dish. Alternatively, strain off the liquid, pat dry with paper towel and seal over a hot chargrill for a smoky finish, and serve with their pickled vegetables.

4 x 120–160 g (4–5½ oz) whole quail
sea salt flakes
145 ml (5 fl oz) extra virgin olive oil
4–6 Dutch carrots, peeled, trimmed and halved
½ small celeriac, cut into 1 cm (½ in) dice
½ fennel, cut into 1 cm (½ in) dice
1 red capsicum (bell pepper), cut into 1 cm (½ in) dice
2 French shallots, thickly sliced
1 garlic bulb, halved crossways

2 fresh bay leaves
1 marjoram or oregano sprig
10 green peppercorns (in brine or dried)
1 pinch of saffron
juice of 1 lemon
250 ml (8½ fl oz/1 cup) dry sherry or dry white wine
60 ml (2 fl oz/¼ cup) sherry or red wine vinegar
250 ml (8½ fl oz/1 cup) chicken stock
freshly ground black pepper

Massage the quail with 1 tablespoon of the oil and sprinkle with a little salt. Heat a large frying pan over high heat, add the quail and seal for 3 minutes on each side or until golden. Transfer to a plate and set aside.

Heat 60 ml (2 fl oz/¼ cup) of the remaining oil in the same pan over medium–high heat. Add the carrot, celeriac, fennel, capsicum, shallot, garlic, bay leaves, marjoram or oregano, green peppercorns and saffron and cook for 5–6 minutes, until the vegetables just start to sweat and soften. Return the quail to the pan, pour in the lemon juice and sherry or wine and bring to a simmer. Add the remaining oil, the vinegar and chicken stock, then cover with a tight-fitting lid, reduce the heat to medium and simmer for 6–8 minutes, until the quail is cooked through.

Transfer the quail, vegetables and liquid to a shallow serving dish and serve straight away or refrigerate overnight and serve with the lentil and goat's cheese salad on page 230 or any salad of your choice.

The pickled quail will keep, covered, in the fridge for 7–10 days, as long as the quail is completely submerged in the pickling liquid.

HERBES

Herb liqueur

If you didn't overdose on it during a trip to the Balearic Islands or you didn't get the chance to purchase any to take back home, try your hand at making your own 'herbes'. This local tipple infuses a bouquet of digestive herbs and botanicals in anise liqueur, giving it a gorgeous transparent green hue with lots of medicinal properties.

You can go foraging in your neighbourhood and mix and match local herbs, but give preference to sweeter plants and add smaller amounts of the stronger botanicals, such as pine and lavender.

2 thick strips of orange peel
2 thick strips of lemon peel
2 fig leaves
2 lavender flowers and stalks
2 pine needle fronds
4 orange leaves
4 lemon leaves
2 fresh bay leaves
2 thyme sprigs
2 rosemary sprigs
2 marjoram or oregano sprigs
2 sage sprigs
2 lemon verbena sprigs
2 mint sprigs
2 pomegranate leaves or flowers
4 fennel or dill fronds and stalks
1 litre (34 fl oz/4 cups) sweet anise liqueur, such as Anis del Mono
500 ml (17 fl oz/2 cups) dry anise liqueur, such as arak

Divide the herbal ingredients between two sterilised 750 ml (25½ fl oz) glass bottles (see Note on page 56), finishing with the fennel fronds.

Mix the alcohols together in a jug and pour over the ingredients. Seal and set aside on a shelf in a cool, dry and dark spot for a minimum of 2 months to infuse its magic.

HOMEMADE

HERBES

This famous liqueur meaning simply 'herbs' connects all the Balearic Islands. It is a simple marriage of foraged spring plants in an aniseed alcohol base. The not-so-famous 'palo' liqueur (meaning stick) is also widespread throughout the islands as the 'vermouth' of the 'Baleares', taken at the beginning of the meal to open the appetite.

A true example of 'terroir' (the 'herbes' from Mallorca and the Pitiuses – Ibiza and Formentera – are Protected Designations of Origin), each island makes their own herb concoctions from locally grown pickings. The drink was traditionally used as a remedy for fever, worms and stomach upsets, but now it's most famously used to combat gluttony thanks to its digestive properties. Although it started out 200 years ago as a home-brew medicine, many families still practise the custom of placing a spring-harvested corsage of local plants in a bottle with anise liqueur, and leaving it to macerate over summer. Every composition is a safely guarded family secret, passed down through the generations as something to share and offer as a pleasing ritual, which is as much for the maker as those who are lucky enough to receive it.

'Herbes' is so embedded in the culture of Balearic Island life that your first and last meal on the islands, and any in between, will always finish with an invitation from the house for a 'xupito de herbes'. Arriving at your table in a small shot glass, three types are usually on offer: sweet, dry and, my favourite, 'mitj I mitj' (half and half). Afterwards, you can buy some at the airport on your way home, in case you haven't had enough of the stuff!

POMADA I PALLOFA

Two gin cocktails

The capital of Menorca, Mahón, is home to the famous Xoriguer Gin. It is a surviving influence from the British occupation of Menorca in the 18th century, and apart from Plymouth it is the only gin with a Protected Designation of Origin. During the occupation, locals used what they had on hand to keep up with the sailors' demand for liquor, and many brewed with distilled wine rather than the usual grains. Xoriguer Gin is still made this way today in wood-fired copper stills, then rested in oak barrels before bottling, which gives it a distinctly bitter and smoky flavour of green wood, juniper and pepper.

These two gin cocktails are served ice-cold on beaches throughout the Balearics. 'Pomada', meaning 'ointment' in Catalan, is made with a cloudy, lemony lemonade and sometimes served as a slushy. For a drier experience, opt for the Pallofa, a beautifully simple gin and soda with a splash of lemon zest.

On the islands, these cocktails contain a 1:1 ratio of gin to mixer, which can all-too-easily be sipped away as a pre-dinner tipple, while sitting at a shaded 'xiringuito' (beach shack). These recipes are toned down a little for when you're not on holiday and have to function the next day!

HOMEMADE

Pomada

135 g (5 oz/1 cup) small-cubed ice
200–250 ml (7–8½ fl oz) good-quality gin
150 ml (5 fl oz) freshly squeezed lemon juice
500–600 ml (17–20½ fl oz) good-quality lemon soda, to taste
2 thick lemon slices, quartered, plus extra slices to serve

Tip the ice into a jug and add the gin and lemon juice. Give everything a stir with a swizzle stick or chopstick, then pour in the lemon soda to taste.

Place two quartered lemon slices in four highball glasses and bruise with a wooden pestle or the end of a wooden spoon. Divide the drink evenly among the glasses and top with a few more slices of lemon. Serve with a little napkin and some salty bar snacks.

Pallofa

200 ml (7 fl oz) good-quality gin
600 ml (20½ fl oz) soda water (club soda)
4 strips of lemon peel
large ice cubes, to serve

Pour the gin into four rocks glasses. Top with the soda water, lemon peel and a few large ice cubes and serve straight away.

SANGRIA DE CIRERA

Cherry sangria

SERVES 8

Thanks to the famous nightlife of Ibiza, the symbol of the double cherry has become a mascot for the island. Couple that with wine in the form of the famous Spanish party tipple sangria, and you have the perfect drink to take you back to that beach-club mood.

The traditional red wine grape varieties of the Balearics are mourvèdre, garnacha and the indigenous callet and manto negro over in Mallorca. They became an important commodity in the 1870s, when the phylloxera virus ravaged vines in mainland Europe, so much so that the wines were shipped to France and relabelled as French!

Today, you'll find foreign varieties, such as cabernet sauvignon and merlot grapes, grown throughout the Balearics where the temperature can be a lot cooler and drier than the mainland. Most of the wine doesn't even leave the islands, as it services the 15 million tourists who visit annually.

180 g (6½ oz) fresh or frozen cherries, pitted and halved
750 ml (25½ fl oz) bottle red wine
200–250 ml (7–8½ fl oz) cherry brandy liqueur, such as kirsch
150 ml (5 fl oz) freshly squeezed orange juice
1 orange, thinly sliced
1 lime, thinly sliced
500–600 ml (17–20½ fl oz) lemon–lime soda
ice cubes, to serve

Combine the cherries, wine, cherry liqueur, orange juice and half the orange and lime slices in a jug. Stir to combine, then refrigerate for at least 2 hours or until completely chilled. Pour in the soda, fill with ice and stir. Evenly divide among eight glasses, top with the remaining orange and lime slices and serve.

HOMEMADE

Cherry sangria

Pomada

Pallofa

CAFÉ CALETA

Mulled Caleta bay coffee

SERVES 8

It's thought that this drink was created by a couple of local fishermen upon their return to Ibiza from compulsory military service in the 50s. They'd been stationed in A Coruña, Galicia, where a similar mulled coffee, 'quiemada', was brewed with the local 'orujo' or 'aguardiente' (firewater). Restaurante Sa Caleta still serves it, burning the cauldron at the table in a theatrical setting, while you sit back digesting a long lunch looking out over burnt-orange cliffs to the greenest of blue Ibizan seas.

50 g (1¾ oz) ground coffee
120 g (4½ oz) raw caster (superfine) sugar
400 ml (13½ fl oz) brandy
400 ml (13½ fl oz) dark rum
2 strips of lemon peel
2 strips of orange peel
2 teaspoons coffee beans
1 cinnamon stick

Tip the coffee into a saucepan and fill with 1.2 litres (41 fl oz) of water. Bring to the boil, then remove from the heat and set aside for 6 minutes to infuse. Strain the liquid through a coffee filter into a jug.

Warm the remaining ingredients in a large heavy-based saucepan or earthenware pot over medium heat, stirring until the sugar has dissolved.

Now for the fun part. Standing back a little, scoop out a large ladleful of liquid and ignite it with a match. Gently lower the lit ladle into the saucepan to set the rest of the liquid alight (keep the lid close by in case you need to quickly smother the flame). Allow the liquid to burn for 3 minutes or until the flame turns blue, then extinguish it by covering with the lid. Stir through the reserved coffee, then ladle into mugs or cups. Serve straight away.

HOMEMADE

he majority of villlagers and townspeople, who once dedicated their lives to working the land for economical gain in agronomy and horticulture, may have been enticed away to the world of tourism and the free market, but traditional harvesting customs still flourish on the Balearic Islands.

Aside from animal husbandry and the fruits of the Mediterranean Sea, there is a bounty of seasonal vegetables grown and consumed on the islands, which make up a large part of the Balearic diet. Wherever there is space and soil, locals attend to these fertile grounds with a focus on conservation and organic growing methods.

Commonly grown fruits and vegetables include 'ramellet' tomatoes (introduced by Spanish conquerors in the 16th century), which are traditionally grown and hung on string, helping to preserve them for winter and selling on to the mainland. Silverbeet (Swiss chard) and eggplants (aubergines) feature heavily, alongside broad (fava) beans, artichokes, capsicums (bell peppers), potatoes, citrus, melons and grapes for wine. Legumes, pulses and grains are also a huge part of the weekly mealtime roster, while honey is still widely used in both sweet and savoury dishes as a garnish.

In addition to refreshing salads and hearty soups, local vegetables are served as snacks or starters, or alongside meat and fish. Each vegetable dish is deeply rooted to 'terroir' and village festivals celebrate their heroes throughout the year, from the mushroom festival of Manacor to the potato fair of Sa Pobla.

The king of Balearic vegetable dishes is the Mallorcan 'tombet' (see page 138). An orchestra of seasonal summer produce from the local vegetable patch, each vegetable is fried separately and then carefully assembled in a single vessel to create a layered savoury cake. If 'tombet' is the king, then the queen is the Ibizan Easter stew 'cuinat' (see page 131), a simple dish consisting of earthy greens and grains. Fresh salads, such as the daintily chopped 'trempó' (see page 121), will often appear on the table, while other fresh produce might be stuffed, used as a topping for the much-loved 'coca' pizza (see page 118), or added to the many soups, stews and stocks made only with local ingredients.

The dishes in this chapter are both rustic and decadent. Cemented in history and tradition, they turn the simple into the delicious through making the most of fresh, seasonal produce, which can be served as a stand-alone meal or alongside any of the savoury dishes in this book.

PA AMB OLI, SOBRASSADA I MEL

Olive oil, sobrassada and honey on toast

SERVES 4

Affectionately pronounced 'pam boli', this simple dish of Mallorcan rye bread (see page 20) and good olive oil is the soulful base of all Balearic Island cooking. It is considered the national breakfast or morning tea, and is always served with olives or pickles on the side. For those with a heavier daily workload ahead of them, cafes also offer the option of adding sobrassada and honey for a more filling meal. These simple and contrasting island flavours – local sweet, floral honey and the intensely strong-flavoured sobrassada – is an exquisite combination unique to the Balearics. You can also use this partnership to baste fish, chicken or stuffed mushrooms or smear atop a canapé or bite-sized piece of toast with a fried quail's egg on top.

½ loaf Mallorcan rye bread (see page 20) or store-bought light rye
4 thick slices sobrassada (see page 216)
1 tablespoon floral honey
olive oil, for drizzling
caper berries, to serve
50 g (1¾ oz) Pickled sea fennel (see page 70)

Preheat a grill (broiler) to high.

Cut the bread into four thick slices and grill on both sides until lightly toasted. Top each piece with a slice of sobrassada and gently spread to the edges. Return the toast to the grill and cook until the sobrassada has melted.

Transfer to plates and drizzle with the honey and oil. Serve with caper berries and pickled sea fennel on the side.

OUS DE SÓLLER

Baked eggs from Sóller

SERVES 4

The modernist town of Sóller in the northwest of Mallorca is described as 'an island within an island'. Once isolated by the Tramuntana mountains, Sóller sits in the heart of the Golden Valley, a large citrus-growing area with a historical trade connection to France via the nearby Port de Sóller.

This French-inspired, yet entirely unique, baked-egg dish is famous throughout Sóller and takes pride of place on every cafe and bar menu, as well as being a favourite in the family home. For a lighter, vegetarian option, omit the sobrassada and add a teaspoon of sweet pimentòn. It still delivers a wonderful flavour that's completely different from the usual tomato and bean base.

1 tablespoon extra virgin olive oil
1 garlic clove, smashed
1 carrot, finely diced
1 celery stalk, finely diced
1 leek, white part only, finely chopped
80 ml (2½ fl oz/⅓ cup) dry white wine or dry sherry
300 ml (10 fl oz) chicken or vegetable stock
500 g (1 lb 2 oz) frozen peas
sea salt flakes and white pepper
4 thick slices sobrassada
8 free-range eggs
crusty bread, to serve

Preheat the oven to 200°C (400°F) fan-forced.

Heat the oil and garlic in a frying pan over medium heat. Add the carrot, celery and leek and cook for 10 minutes or until the vegetables are just beginning to colour and soften. Splash the wine into the pan and simmer until the liquid evaporates, then pour in the stock and bring to the boil. Reduce the heat and simmer for 5 minutes.

Stir all but 50 g (1¾ oz) of the peas into the pan and cook for 1 minute. Remove from the heat and season to taste with salt and white pepper. Transfer the mixture to a blender and blend to a smooth purée.

Pass the pea purée through a fine sieve into a bowl, then transfer the bowl to an ice bath, stirring to release the heat (this helps to maintain the green colour).

Place the sobrassada along one side of a large pie dish (or two smaller dishes) and spoon in enough purée to just cover the base of the rest of the dish. Crack the eggs on top of the pea purée and sprinkle over the remaining peas. Cover with a lid or foil and bake for 6–8 minutes for a soft yolk or 10 minutes if you prefer your eggs well done.

Meanwhile, reheat the remaining purée. Spoon the purée over the baked eggs, sprinkle with a little more pepper and serve with a big chunk of crusty bread on the side.

VILLAGE

ESCUDELLA FRESCA

Mallorcan minestrone

SERVES 4–6

Unlike, but not dissimilar to, the Catalan Christmas version of 'escudella', this minestrone is made all year round with fresh seasonal legumes instead of dried. In winter, it might also be made with pumpkin and potato, but come early spring the markets are bursting with fresh produce, such as broad (fava) beans, borlotti beans, peas and runner (flat) beans. Traditionally, Mallorcan 'escudella' also includes local charcuterie, such as botifarró (black pudding), blanquet (white pudding), camaïot and xuia (pancetta).

2 tomatoes
1½ tablespoons extra virgin olive oil
150 g (5½ oz) pancetta or streaky bacon, finely chopped
4 spring onions (scallions), finely chopped
3 garlic cloves, finely chopped
6 Dutch carrots, sliced into 1.5 cm (½ in) thick rounds
1 celery stalk, cut into 1.5 cm (½ in) dice
½ fennel bulb, cut into 1.5 cm (½ in) dice
4 marjoram or oregano sprigs

1 strip of lemon peel, white pith removed
2 fresh bay leaves
1 litre (34 fl oz/4 cups) vegetable or chicken stock
100 g (3½ oz) runner (flat) beans, trimmed and cut into 4 cm (1½ in) lengths
80 g (2¾ oz/½ cup) frozen peas
100 g (3½ oz) frozen broad (fava) beans, thawed and double-podded
sea salt flakes and freshly ground black pepper
½ bunch chives, finely snipped

Using a sharp knife, score a cross in the base of the tomatoes. Bring a saucepan of water to the boil and blanch the tomatoes for 2 minutes or until the skins start to curl away from the flesh. Immediately drain and plunge into iced water, then peel away the skins and cut the flesh into quarters. Remove and discard the seeds, then cut the quarters in half and set aside.

Heat the oil in a large saucepan over medium–high heat. Add the pancetta and cook for 4–5 minutes, until golden brown, then add the spring onion and garlic and cook, stirring, for 3–4 minutes, until the spring onion has softened. Add the chopped tomato and cook, stirring, for 2 minutes, then reduce the heat to medium–low and add the carrot, celery, fennel, marjoram or oregano, lemon peel and bay leaves. Cook, stirring occasionally, for 8–10 minutes, until the vegetables are soft but not caramelised.

Pour in the stock, cover with a lid and increase the heat to high. Remove the lid as soon as the mixture starts to boil and add the beans, peas and broad beans. Simmer for 4–6 minutes, until the beans are cooked through, then remove from the heat and season to taste with salt and pepper.

Ladle the minestrone into serving bowls and serve, garnished with the chives.

SOPES SEQUES (SOPAS MALLORQUINAS)

Mallorcan bread soup

SERVES 4–6

'Sopas mallorquinas' is another soup where the ingredients change with the seasons, but one constant you will always find is thin slices of local farmhouse bread. This is essentially a hearty vegetable-based soup that's often made without meat, as the bread contributes so much texture to this much-loved Mallorcan family favourite that's been passed down the generations.

½ loaf Mallorcan rye bread (see page 20) or
    store-bought light rye
2 tomatoes
1½ tablespoons extra virgin olive oil,
    plus extra for drizzling
150 g (5½ oz) piece pork spare ribs, roughly
    chopped into 1 cm (½ in) pieces
1 tablespoon sobrassada (see page 216)
1 leek, white part only, finely chopped
3 garlic cloves, finely chopped
¼ head of cauliflower, cut into small florets

200 g (7 oz) shredded savoy cabbage
4 marjoram or oregano sprigs
2 teaspoons sweet pimentòn
1 litre (34 fl oz/4 cups) vegetable or
    chicken stock
100 g (3½ oz) green beans, trimmed, cut
    into 2.5 cm (1 in) lengths
150 g (5½ oz) baby English spinach leaves
sea salt flakes and freshly ground black pepper
½ bunch chives, finely snipped

Preheat the oven to 170°C (340°F) fan-forced.

Place the bread in the freezer for 30–60 minutes to harden a little before slicing. Using a sharp bread knife, slice the bread as thinly as possible, then transfer to a baking tray in a single layer and bake for 6 minutes to dry out.

Using a sharp knife, score a cross in the base of the tomatoes. Bring a saucepan of water to the boil and blanch the tomatoes for 2 minutes or until the skins start to curl away from the flesh. Immediately drain and plunge into iced water, then peel away the skins and cut the flesh into quarters. Remove and discard the seeds and roughly chop the flesh.

Heat the oil in a large saucepan over medium–high heat. Add the pork ribs and cook for 4–5 minutes, until golden brown all over, then add the sobrassada, leek and garlic and cook, stirring, for 3–4 minutes, until the leeks soften slightly. Add the chopped tomato and cook, stirring, for 2 minutes, then reduce the heat to medium–low and add the cauliflower, cabbage, marjoram or oregano and pimentòn. Cook for 8–10 minutes, until the vegetables are soft but not caramelised.

Pour in the stock, cover with a lid and increase the heat to high. Remove the lid as soon as the mixture starts to boil and add the beans. Simmer for 4–6 minutes, until the beans are cooked through, then remove from the heat, stir through the spinach and season to taste with salt and pepper.

Ladle the soup into bowls and gently place the bread slices on top. Drizzle with a little oil and serve, garnished with the chives.

OLIAIGUA AMB TOMÀTIGA

Menorcan tomato soup

SERVES 4

With very few ingredients, this traditional peasant dish from Menorca depends upon the ripeness and quality of the tomatoes, capsicums and even garlic. It's served with figs on the side – which you eat simultaneously with the soup – a little extra onion and chargrilled bread, which adds a lovely smoky flavour. The soup can be served hot, cold or at room temperature.

1 kg (2 lb 3 oz) ripe tomatoes
1 tablespoon extra-virgin olive oil,
    plus extra for drizzling
2 garlic cloves, peeled
1 green capsicum (bell pepper), thinly sliced
2 salad onions, sliced into rings
1 tablespoon sherry vinegar
sea salt flakes
8 thin slices sourdough
4 figs, to serve

Using a sharp knife, score a cross in the base of the tomatoes. Bring a saucepan of water to the boil and blanch the tomatoes for 2 minutes or until the skins start to curl away from the flesh. Immediately drain and plunge into iced water, then peel away the skins and roughly chop the flesh.

Heat the oil and garlic in a large saucepan over medium heat and cook for about 3 minutes, until the garlic is golden on all sides. Add the tomato, capsicum and half the onion. Increase the heat to medium–high and cook, stirring occasionally, for 15 minutes or until the capsicum is soft. Add 1.5 litres (51 fl oz/6 cups) of water, then reduce the heat to medium–low and simmer for 20 minutes.

Meanwhile, place the remaining onion, the sherry vinegar, 100 ml (3½ fl oz) of water and a pinch of salt in a small bowl. Set aside for 10 minutes, then strain off the liquid and transfer the onion to a small serving bowl.

Heat a chargrill pan over medium heat and toast the bread on both sides until slightly charred. Place in the base of each serving bowl.

Just before serving, find the garlic cloves in the soup and squash them with the back of a spoon to incorporate into the mixture. Ladle the soup over the bread, top with a few slices of macerated onion and drizzle over a little oil. Serve with the figs and remaining onion on the table.

FAVA PARADA

Braised broad beans with fideos

SERVES 4–6

'Fava parada' is Mallorcan through and through. This heavy winter staple with black
pudding, pasta and dried broad (fava) beans can be as sophisticated or simple as you like.
I've used unpeeled broad beans in this recipe, which makes a much chunkier version, but
I love how they allow me to chew my way through this substantial meal. Other versions
involve simply blitzing the cooked beans with a good stock before adding the pasta.
However it is made, come winter, this is what Mallorcans crave.

2 tablespoons extra virgin olive oil, plus extra for drizzling
1 leek, white part only, finely chopped
3 garlic cloves, crushed
50 g (1¾ oz) sobrassada, fresh minced (ground) chorizo or 1 teaspoon sweet pimentòn
50 g (1¾ oz) black pudding, de-cased
3 tomatoes, halved and grated, skins discarded
2 litres (2 qts) vegetable or chicken stock
1 small pig's trotter, halved (ask your butcher to do this for you) or 1 pig's ear
300 g (10½ oz) dried broad (fava) beans, soaked in cold water overnight, drained
250 g (9 oz) pork spare ribs
150 g (5½ oz) thick fideo pasta or spaghetti no. 5, cut into 4 cm (1½ in) lengths
1 teaspoon marjoram or oregano leaves
sea salt flakes and freshly ground black pepper
crusty bread, to serve

Heat the oil, leek and garlic in a large heavy-based saucepan over medium–low heat.
Cook, stirring occasionally, for 6–8 minutes until the leek begins to soften. Stir through
the sobrassada and black pudding and cook for 3 minutes, then add the grated tomato
and cook for 6–8 minutes, until the tomato has reduced and darkened in colour.

Increase the heat to medium, then pour in the stock and add the pig's trotter and broad
beans. Bring to a simmer and cook, semi-covered, for 50–60 minutes, until reduced.
Add the pork spare ribs and poach for 15 minutes or until cooked through. Remove the
spare ribs from the pan and cut into even chunks. Return the ribs to the pan, add the
fideo pasta and marjoram or oregano and simmer for 10–12 minutes, until the pasta
is cooked through.

Season to taste with salt and plenty of pepper and serve it up with some crusty bread
and a drizzle of oil.

VILLAGE

BUNYOLS DE BLEDES

Silverbeet doughnuts

MAKES 10–15

These bite-sized Menorcan joys are traditionally served as a dessert, but adding a little garlic and cumin turns them into a really quirky starter or appetiser. Add a squeeze of lemon at the end, along with a sprinkling of salt and a drizzle of honey, and your guests will start to wonder what stage of the meal they're at! And if you're still hungry after an evening of feasting, you can have one for dessert as well. If there's any left . . .

300 g (10½ oz) silverbeet (Swiss chard), stalks removed
150 g (5½ oz/1 cup) plain (all-purpose) flour
2 free-range eggs
150 ml (5 fl oz) full-cream (whole) milk
1 tablespoon caster (superfine) sugar
½ teaspoon baking powder
2 garlic cloves, crushed
large handful of parsley, leaves finely chopped
½ teaspoon ground cumin
sea salt flakes and freshly ground black pepper
1 litre (34 fl oz/4 cups) vegetable oil
2 tablespoons honey
juice of ½ lemon
your favourite hard cheese, to serve
Grandma's smashed olives (see page 73), to serve

Slice the silverbeet leaves as thinly as possible. Rinse well in iced water, then drain and set aside on a clean tea towel to dry.

Combine the flour, eggs, milk, sugar and baking powder in a bowl to make a batter. Fold through the garlic, parsley, cumin, a pinch of salt and pepper and the silverbeet, then set aside for 10 minutes.

Heat the oil in a large heavy-based saucepan to 180°C (350°F) on a kitchen thermometer. Working in batches, spoon tablespoons of the batter into the oil and fry for 2–3 minutes on each side until golden (they are so light, they usually turn themselves over). Using a slotted spoon, transfer the doughnuts to a tray lined with paper towel.

Place the doughnuts on a large serving plate, sprinkle with some extra salt and drizzle over the honey and lemon. Serve with a big slab of your favourite hard cheese and a few olives, and get ready to lick your fingers.

CARXOFES ARREBOSSADES

Beer-battered artichoke chips

SERVES 4–6

Originally from Andalucia, these addictive morsels get washed down all summer long throughout the Balearics in 'xiringuitos' (beach-bar shacks) and by hotel pools with a beer or two between dips. I love scooping them up with a really hot English mustard 'allioli', which is also popular with the German and British tourists who, along with beer, both love a spicy condiment!

8–10 small artichokes, hard outer leaves removed
fine sea salt
1 lemon, halved
150 g (5½ oz/1 cup) plain (all-purpose) flour
90 g (3 oz/½ cup) potato or rice flour
½ teaspoon baking powder
250 ml (8½ fl oz/1 cup) ice-cold lager
1 free-range egg
1 litre (34 fl oz/4 cups) vegetable oil
sea salt flakes
unpitted black olives, to serve

Mustard allioli
2 garlic cloves
80 g (2½ oz) good-quality egg mayonnaise
2 teaspoons hot English mustard

Trim the artichoke stalks, leaving 2 cm (¾ in) of stalk attached. Peel the outer layer of the stalks with a vegetable peeler.

Bring a large saucepan of water to the boil and season well with salt. Add the trimmed artichokes and one lemon half squeezed in, and blanch for 6–8 minutes, until the artichokes are just under-cooked and still a little firm. Remove from the pan and pat dry with a clean tea towel, squeezing out as much moisture as possible. Discard the lemon.

Cut the artichokes in half and remove the fibrous choke, then cut into 5 mm (¼ in) thick slices.

Combine half the plain flour, the potato or rice flour, baking powder and ½ teaspoon of fine sea salt in a large bowl. Slowly pour in the beer, whisking continuously to avoid any lumps, then beat in the egg until the batter has a thick cream consistency.

Heat the oil in a large frying pan to 180°C (350°F) on a kitchen thermometer.

Meanwhile, make the mustard allioli. In a small bowl, finely grate the garlic into the mayonnaise and stir through the mustard. Set aside.

Dust the artichoke slices with the remaining plain flour, then dip in the batter to coat. Working in batches, fry the artichoke for 2–3 minutes, until golden, then transfer to a tray lined with paper towel and sprinkle with salt flakes before the excess oil dries off.

Serve the artichoke chips with the mustard allioli and a few olives on the side.

TRUITA DE BOLETS I BLEDES

Wild mushroom and silverbeet omelette

SERVES 4

After all the summer 'guiri' (tourists) have left, the islands breathe again and mushroom spores eject under fallen logs in the humid forests. Foraging for mushrooms is a popular family tradition on the islands and there are over one hundred edible varieties. The most common mushrooms served on menus and sold in markets at the beginning of autumn are white saddle, black trompettes, coral mushrooms and the 'l'esclata-sang' or red pine, a mushroom so revered that in the town of Mancor de la Vall in Mallorca, a three-day festival is dedicated to this humble fungus.

The combination of egg, mushroom and silverbeet in this recipe is soulful, earthy and grounding. Feel free to mix up the mushrooms with whatever is available at your local market, but do try and use different colours and textures.

2 teaspoons butter
1 tablespoon extra virgin olive oil
1 salad onion, sliced
400 g (14 oz) mixed mushrooms, roughly chopped
2 garlic cloves, finely chopped
1 thyme sprig
125 ml (4 fl oz/½ cup) dry sherry or dry white wine
8 silverbeet (Swiss chard) leaves, stalks removed, larger leaves cut in half
8 large free-range eggs, lightly beaten
crusty bread, to serve

Heat the butter and oil in a large (or two medium) heavy-based frying pan over medium–high heat. Add the onion and cook for 4–6 minutes, until translucent and starting to soften. Add the mushroom, garlic, thyme and sherry, increase the heat to high and cook, stirring continuously, for 6–8 minutes, until the mushroom is golden and tender.

Add the silverbeet leaves and pour in the beaten egg. Reduce the heat to low and stir until the egg starts to scramble. Using a spatula, evenly distribute the egg throughout the mushroom and silverbeet mixture. Cover the pan and cook for 3–4 minutes, until the egg is cooked and golden on the base, but still quite moist in the middle.

Serve with a big chunk of crusty bread.

COCA TREMPÓ

Balearic pizza

SERVES 6–8

This rustic classic was traditionally made on bread-making day as a way to use up extra dough and yeast, while any left-over late summer vegetables from the local 'trempó' salad (see page 121) were used for the topping. A field-worker's recipe that took advantage of excess produce at harvest, 'coca trempó' was free, quick to make and easy to transport back to the fields where the workers tilled under the hot island sun.

Use any left-over (or make extra) 'trempó' to top this biscuity base. The cooked apple on this pizza is a revelation!

180 ml (6 fl oz) lukewarm water
2½ teaspoons dry active yeast
2 tablespoons extra virgin olive oil, plus extra for greasing
½ teaspoon caster (superfine) sugar
350 g (12½ oz) plain (all-purpose) flour, plus extra for dusting
½ teaspoon fine sea salt
1 tablespoon softened lard or olive oil
½ quantity Trempó (see page 121)
freshly ground black pepper

Line a 25 x 38 cm (10 x 15¼ in) baking tray with baking paper and lightly grease with oil.

Combine the water, yeast, extra virgin olive oil and the sugar in a small jug and set aside to activate for 5–8 minutes at room temperature.

Place the flour and salt in a large bowl. Once the yeast mixture starts to froth, slowly mix it into the flour until a rough dough forms. Transfer the dough to a well-floured work surface and knead for 5 minutes or until you have a smooth but firm dough. Place the dough on the prepared tray, cover with a clean and ever-so-slightly damp tea towel and leave to rest at room temperature for 15–20 minutes, until it has risen by one-third.

On a lightly floured work surface, roll the dough into a 6 mm (¼ in) thick rectangle that's roughly the same size as your baking tray. Carefully transfer the dough to the tray and gently push the dough to the corners of the tray. Cover with the tea towel and set aside to rest for 30 minutes.

Preheat the oven to 200°C (400°F) fan-forced.

Lightly brush the dough with the lard or oil and arrange the trempó mix in an even layer over the dough. Transfer to the oven and bake for 20–25 minutes, until golden and cooked through. Remove from the oven and season generously with freshly ground black pepper.

Cut the pizza into random-sized pieces and eat straight off the tray, or take it down to the beach for a snack between swims.

TREMPÓ

Chopped Mallorcan salad

SERVES 4–6

I used to serve this dish at The Spanish Club in Melbourne, way back when it was heaving with live music, locals and club members. It's still one of my all-time favourite salads, especially when the vegetables are picked straight from the summer garden. I love that you can have one of every ingredient in your mouth at once – it's like your very own salad bowl in every spoonful!

The trick here is to dice everything the same size – no bigger than your fingernails – and to use the best cold-pressed extra virgin olive oil you can get your hands on. I've added apple to this dish, which isn't traditional, but the freshness of it is the best surprise on a hot summer's day. I also sometimes add red chilli, especially when I'm drinking a good rosé to wash it down with.

1 white onion, diced
1 granny smith apple, peeled, cored and diced
juice of ½ lemon
1 small green bullhorn pepper, diced
1 small red capsicum (bell pepper), diced
1 small yellow capsicum (bell pepper), diced
2 vine-ripened tomatoes, diced
2½ tablespoons extra virgin olive oil
1½ tablespoons sherry vinegar
1 teaspoon cumin seeds, toasted and ground
½ teaspoon sweet pimentòn
sea salt flakes and freshly ground black pepper
3 marjoram or oregano sprigs, leaves picked
crusty bread, to serve
Grandma's smashed olives (see page 73), to serve (optional)

Place the white onion in a small bowl of iced water and combine the apple and lemon juice in another bowl. Set aside for 10 minutes, then drain.

Combine the pepper, capsicums, tomato, oil, vinegar, cumin and pimentòn in a serving bowl, then add the onion and apple. Season with salt and pepper, to taste and scatter over the marjoram or oregano leaves.

Serve with crusty bread and some smashed olives on the side, if you like.

AMANIDA DE CROSTES

Island panzanella

SERVES 4–6

Never mind about not eating your crusts – this is the salad of crusts! This refreshing side dish from Formentera and Ibiza was traditionally made by fishermen using the ends of left-over bread. The men would take the bread with them on long hauls at sea, where they would make this salad, along with the fish they caught.

Day-old bread is best, but it's not imperative. If you do use stale bread, rehydrate it with a sprinkling of water before baking, to get it even drier and less chewy. This allows the bread to better absorb the vinaigrette, while keeping that crunchy texture alive.

450 g (1 lb) day-old crusty bread, ripped into bite-sized chunks
1 white onion, thinly sliced into rings
2½ tablespoons extra virgin olive oil, plus extra for drizzling
1½ tablespoons sherry vinegar
1 small green capsicum (bell pepper), very finely diced
2 garlic cloves, thinly sliced
small pinch of caster (superfine) sugar
500 g (1 lb 2 oz) mixed tomatoes, roughly chopped or sliced
sea salt flakes and freshly ground black pepper
6 tinned sardines or large anchovy fillets
6 caper berries, halved
3 parsley sprigs, roughly chopped

Preheat the oven to 180°C (350°F) fan-forced.

Place the bread on a baking tray in a single layer and lightly sprinkle with water (or use a spray bottle if you have one). Transfer to the oven and bake for 20 minutes or until lightly toasted and completely dry.

Place the white onion in a bowl of iced water and set aside for 10 minutes.

Mix the oil, vinegar, capsicum, garlic and sugar in a small bowl to make a dressing.

Drain the onion and place in a mixing bowl with the toasted bread, tomato and dressing. Season with salt and pepper and toss well for 1 minute or so to combine, making sure the bread is completely coated in the dressing. Scatter over the sardines or anchovies, caper berries and parsley, and serve immediately.

VILLAGE

PATATA I MAHONESA

Mayonnaise potatoes

SERVES 4–6

Menorca, or more specifically its capital Mahón, has often laid claim to the origins of the most famous condiment in the world: the universally loved 'mayo'. The Spanish claim that the French stole it during their occupation of the island in the mid 1700s, and that they then ran away with it, changed the spelling and popularised it around the globe.

For this salad, I like to leave the potato skins on for colour and taste. Double the potato recipe for a larger feast, which also helps you use up more of the 'mahonesa'. Alternatively, it will keep in an airtight container in the fridge for up to a week.

30 g (1 oz/¼ cup) raisins, roughly chopped
2 tablespoons sherry vinegar
1 kg (2 lb 3 oz) chat (baby) potatoes
1 tablespoon extra virgin olive oil
1 salad onion, chopped
30 g (1 oz/¼ cup) slivered almonds, toasted
6 parsley sprigs, finely chopped
¼ bunch dill, fronds picked and finely chopped
3 tarragon sprigs, leaves picked, plus extra to serve
sea salt flakes and freshly ground black pepper

Mahonesa
1 free-range egg yolk
1 free-range egg
1 tablespoon sherry vinegar
1 teaspoon freshly squeezed lemon juice
pinch of sea salt flakes
160 ml (5½ fl oz) grapeseed oil
160 ml (5½ fl oz) extra virgin olive oil

Heat the raisins and sherry vinegar in a small saucepan over medium heat for 2–3 minutes. Set aside.

To make the mahonesa, place the egg yolk and egg in a mixing bowl or in the bowl of a food processor. Whisk or blitz to combine, then incorporate the vinegar, lemon juice and salt. Whisking or blitzing continuously, very gradually pour in the oils, one at a time, in a thin, steady stream, until you have a thick mayonnaise.

Place the potatoes in a large saucepan of salted water and bring to the boil. Cook for 25–30 minutes, until tender but not falling apart. Drain and transfer to a large bowl with the oil and vinegared raisins and their juice. Stir well to coat the potatoes, then set aside for 20 minutes or so before adding the remaining ingredients and mixing through as much mahonesa as you like. Sprinkle with a few extra tarragon leaves and serve.

COLIFLOR OFEGADA

Cauliflower braise

SERVES 4–6

This dish is associated with a distinct cooking technique called 'sacsejar', meaning to shake. In Mallorca, it's a very typical way to cook, sweating down the ingredients in a large tightly sealed stockpot, almost like a pressure cooker but without the accelerated pressure! As the ingredients cook, you shake the pot from side to side to mix the contents, all the while retaining the steam and avoiding mashing up the ingredients with a spoon.

Traditionally, this dish is served with sliced black pudding on the side, but it's equally delicious on its own.

2 tomatoes
1½ tablespoons extra virgin olive oil
150 g (5½ oz) pancetta or streaky bacon, roughly chopped
2 teaspoons aniseed or fennel seeds
4–5 spring onions (scallions), chopped
3 garlic cloves, finely chopped
1 head of cauliflower, cut into small florets
1 teaspoon sweet pimentòn, plus extra for dusting
30 g (1 oz/¼ cup) raisins, roughly chopped
30 g (1 oz) pine nuts, toasted
sea salt flakes and freshly ground black pepper
4 parsley sprigs, chopped

Using a sharp knife, score a cross in the base of the tomatoes. Bring a saucepan of water to the boil and blanch the tomatoes for 2 minutes or until the skins start to curl away from the flesh. Immediately drain and plunge into iced water, then peel away the skins and cut the flesh into quarters. Remove and discard the seeds, then finely dice the flesh and set aside.

Heat the oil in a large stockpot over medium–high heat. Add the pancetta and cook for 4–5 minutes, until golden, then add the aniseed, spring onion and garlic and cook, stirring, for 3–4 minutes, until the spring onion has softened. Stir through the chopped tomato and cook for 2 minutes. Reduce the heat to medium–low, add the cauliflower, pimentòn, raisins and pine nuts and stir well to combine.

To create a tight seal for your pot, wrap the lid in at least one thick tea towel. Cover the pot with the wrapped lid and cook for 5 minutes. 'Sacsejar' the pot from time to time by shaking it from side to side, holding the lid tightly as you slide the pan back and forth over the burner. Open the lid to check if the ingredients are catching on the bottom and reduce the heat if so. Replace the lid and continue cooking for a further 15 minutes, carefully shaking the pot every 3 minutes or so.

Transfer the braised cauliflower to a serving dish, season to taste with salt and pepper and serve with a little freshly chopped parsley sprinkled over the top.

CUINAT

Ibizan Easter stew with greens, broad beans and mint

SERVES 4–6

I love this dish, but I can imagine being a kid and having to eat it every year for Lent would have been a chore, given all the hearty vegetables. Adults, however, are very fond of this national pride on a plate, so much so, that not even the tourists know about it.

The greens in this recipe are traditionally from the *Silene vulgaris* plant – a local edible weed native to Europe, but I've used chrysanthemum as a floral, bitey and herbaceous substitute. You can also use leaf chicory (or both), which is slightly more bitter.

The dried lupin bean 'almortas' – an animal feed crop on Mallorca – can also be attributed to the roots of this festive dish. You can use dried broad (fava) beans instead, but I find the nuttiness of the yellow split pea a perfect substitute for the lupin, plus they're speedier to cook!

200 g (7 oz/1 cup) yellow split peas
1 bunch silverbeet (Swiss chard)
2 tablespoons extra virgin olive oil, plus
    extra for drizzling
2 onions, finely diced
8 garlic cloves, crushed
3 tomatoes, grated, skins discarded
pinch of saffron
2 teaspoons sweet pimentòn
1 teaspoon dried mint

2 young garlic shoots, sliced (omit
    if unavailable)
250 ml (8½ fl oz/1 cup) vegetable stock
zest and juice of 1 lemon
sea salt flakes and freshly ground black pepper
150 g (5½ oz) double-podded broad (fava)
    beans, roughly chopped
200 g (7 oz) chrysanthemum or leaf chicory,
    leaves stripped and roughly chopped
3 mint sprigs, leaves picked and thinly sliced

Rinse the split peas under cold running water, then place in a large saucepan with twice the amount of water as the peas. Bring to the boil over medium–high heat and cook for 30–40 minutes, until tender. Drain and set aside.

Pull the silverbeet leaves from their stalks and finely chop them both, reserving them separately.

Heat the oil in a large frying pan over medium–high heat. Add the onion and cook for 6 minutes or until beginning to soften. Add the silverbeet stalks and garlic and stir well to combine. Cook for 3–4 minutes, then add the tomato, saffron, pimentòn, dried mint and young garlic shoots, if using. Stir for 3–4 minutes, then pour in the stock and bring to a simmer. Cook for 5–6 minutes, then add the split peas and lemon zest.

Continue to cook until the split peas are heated through, then season to taste and stir in the silverbeet leaves, broad beans and chrysanthemum or chicory. Cook until the leaves are wilted, then check the seasoning and adjust, if necessary.

Transfer the stew to a serving bowl and squeeze over the lemon juice. Scatter over the mint leaves, along with a big drizzle of oil and plenty of freshly ground black pepper.

VERDURES FARCIDES

Stuffed vegetables

SERVES 4

Stuffed vegetables are iconic throughout the Mediterranean islands. From Cyprus in the east and the neighbouring Aegean Islands, to Malta, Corsica, Sardinia and, of course, the Balearics, they all have a signature recipe for hulling out various whole vegetables and stuffing them with an array of delectable ingredients. As a point of difference from its Mediterranean island cousins, this classic Balearic version uses sobrassada and fennel.

2 potatoes, halved
2 zucchini (courgettes), halved lengthways
2 long thin eggplants (aubergines), halved lengthways
2½ tablespoons extra virgin olive oil
1 onion, finely diced
2 garlic cloves, finely chopped
1 teaspoon fennel seeds
1 teaspoon allspice
1 teaspoon finely chopped rosemary leaves
150 g (5½ oz) lean minced (ground) pork
250 g (9 oz) lean minced (ground) beef
100 g (3½ oz) sobrassada or minced (ground) chorizo
sea salt flakes
3 marjoram or oregano sprigs, leaves chopped
freshly ground black pepper
250 ml (8½ fl oz/1 cup) passata (puréed tomatoes)
2 slices fresh bread, blitzed in a food processor

Preheat the oven to 200°C (400°F) fan-forced. Line a deep baking dish with baking paper.

Place the potato in a large saucepan of salted water and bring to the boil. Cook for 4 minutes, then drain and set aside until cool enough to handle. Spoon out the potato flesh, leaving a 1 cm (½ in) layer of potato around the edges and base. Discard the potato flesh or save for another use.

Spoon out the zucchini and eggplant flesh in the same way, then finely chop the flesh and set aside.

Heat the oil in a large heavy-based saucepan over medium–high heat. Add the onion and garlic and cook, stirring, for 10 minutes or until soft and golden. Stir through the fennel, allspice and rosemary and cook for 2 minutes.

Add the minced pork and beef, sobrassada, a pinch of salt and the chopped zucchini and eggplant and cook for 10 minutes, breaking up any lumps with the back of a wooden spoon, or until the meat has browned and any liquid has evaporated.

Transfer the mixture to a large bowl and set aside to cool a little before adding the marjoram and seasoning with salt and pepper.

Spoon the mixture into the hollowed-out vegetables and place in the lined baking dish.

Spoon 1–2 tablespoons of passata over the top of each stuffed vegetable half, then sprinkle over the breadcrumbs and bake for 10–12 minutes, until golden.

CANELONS DE ALBERGINES

Eggplant canelones

MAKES 12

The combination of nightshade ingredients in this dish shows how sophisticated peasant food can be, with its signature island flavours of sweet and savoury potato, floral honey, bitter and creamy eggplant and a touch of cinnamon.

In Ibiza, I served a wood-fired version of this dish with grapes and purslane given to me by a local market gardener who grew them in his front yard in the neighbouring town of Jesus. In this recipe, I've mixed up the typical Mediterranean stuffed–vegetable repertoire by turning the canelones into an appetiser that's great for handing round at dinner parties.

2 eggplants (aubergines), cut lengthways
  into 5 mm (¼ in) thick slices
2 teaspoons fine sea salt
750 g (1 lb 11 oz) large desiree potatoes, peeled
60 g (2 oz) butter
3 tablespoons extra virgin olive oil
1½ tablespoons pure cream

½ teaspoon ground cinnamon,
  plus extra for dusting
2 thyme sprigs, leaves chopped super fine
sea salt flakes and freshly ground black pepper
80 g (2½ oz) slivered almonds, finely chopped
3 tablespoons honey
5 purslane or ice plant sprigs, leaves picked

Place the eggplant in a large colander with a bowl underneath and sprinkle over the fine sea salt. Set aside for 6–8 minutes to draw out the eggplant's bitter juices. Rinse off the salt and squeeze the slices dry with a clean tea towel, removing as much moisture as possible.

Place the potatoes in a large saucepan of salted water and bring to the boil. Cook for 25–30 minutes, until tender but not falling apart. Drain and push the potato through a ricer, mouli or fine sieve into a large bowl. While the potato is still warm, add half the butter, 1 tablespoon of the oil, the cream, cinnamon and thyme. Season with salt and pepper and mix well, beating with a wooden spoon. Set aside to cool, then refrigerate for 20 minutes.

Preheat the oven to 180°C (350°F) fan-forced. Line a baking tray with baking paper.

Heat a small drizzle of the remaining oil in a large heavy-based frying pan over medium–high heat. Working in batches, cook the eggplant slices, drizzling with oil each time, for 2–3 minutes on each side until golden brown. Drain on paper towel to absorb any excess oil.

Once cool enough to handle, place the eggplant on a chopping board and spoon 1½ tablespoons of the mashed potato mixture in a thick horizontal line across each eggplant slice. Roll up from the round bottom end of the eggplant and set aside on the prepared tray, seam side down.

Melt the remaining butter and use it to baste the tops of the canelones. Sprinkle over the almonds and bake for 12–15 minutes, until warmed through and the almonds are golden brown.

Transfer the canelones to a large serving platter and drizzle with honey just before serving. Sprinkle over a very fine amount of cinnamon and season with salt and pepper. Finish with the purslane leaves and serve.

EGGPLAN

Inherited by the Moors via India and taken to Spain, the unassuming eggplant (aubergine) thrives on the Balearic Islands with its mild climate, plenty of warmth and humidity. Locals are very fond of this summer vegetable (there's even a popular restaurant in Ibiza called Aubergine) and always seem to know how to transform it into something special. It often appears alongside its nightshade cousins, potato, capsicum (bell pepper) and tomato, and even if you are indifferent to eggplant, you will discover how versatile these little island jewels are through some of the islands' long-established favourite dishes.

From the more traditional recipes that bake eggplant in milk, to omelettes, terrines and tarts or even sweetened eggplants used in a dessert, there is many a use for this summer friend. Stuffed is probably the most common go-to preparation for many households (see page 132), as it makes a quick and easy dinner. Some like to roast or boil their eggplants first, while others prefer to fill them with the scooped-out vegetable flesh or with fish. They might then be crumbed and fried or simply baked in the oven for a lovely toasty finish.

Other popular dishes include the quirky rolled canelones filled with cinnamon-infused mashed potato (see page 135) or as pride of place among the orchestra of vegetables in the famous Mallorcan 'tombet' (see page 138).

TOMBET

Roasted vegetable claypot

SERVES 4

Like French ratatouille, Spanish pisto and Catalan samfaina, the Balearic Islands have their own version of slow-cooked vegetables. With the addition of potato, the ingredients are roasted in the oven in this elegant version, which is humbly satisfying, especially when made with good-quality summer produce from the garden or local neighbourhood. Mallorcans serve this classic as an appetiser or in the centre of the table as an accompaniment to fish or meat. There is often no need for forks, as it just gets scooped up with a slice of local bread, bypassing even the plate. You might want to wear a bib if you want to experience it this way!

1 kg (2 lb 3 oz) ripe roma (plum) tomatoes
sea salt flakes and freshly ground black pepper
2 teaspoons dried oregano
3 fresh bay leaves
½ teaspoon caster (superfine) sugar
2 medium eggplants (aubergines), sliced into 2 cm (¾ in) thick rounds
2 teaspoons fine sea salt
250 ml (8½ fl oz/1 cup) extra virgin olive oil
400 g (14 oz) potatoes, peeled, sliced into 1.5 cm (½ in) thick rounds

1 large zucchini (courgette), sliced into 2 cm (¾ in) thick rounds
1 red capsicum (bell pepper), sliced into 2 cm (¾ in) thick rings
1 green capsicum (bell pepper), sliced into 2 cm (¾ in) thick rings
1 red onion, sliced into 2 cm (¾ in) thick rings
3 garlic cloves, thinly sliced
3 tablespoons honey
80 g (2¾ oz) walnuts, chopped

Cut the tomatoes in half and grate the cut side, using the skin as a handle. Discard the skins and place the grated tomato in a fine sieve over a bowl to drain off some of the liquid. Transfer to a bowl, season with salt and pepper and mix through the oregano, bay leaves and sugar.

Place the eggplant in a large colander with a bowl underneath and sprinkle over the fine sea salt. Set aside for 6–8 minutes to draw out the eggplant's bitter juices. Rinse off the salt and squeeze the slices dry with a clean tea towel, removing as much moisture as possible.

Heat the oil in a large heavy-based frying pan over medium heat. Add the potato and cook on each side for 8–12 minutes, until golden and cooked through. Transfer to a large plate lined with paper towel to absorb the excess oil. Repeat this process for each vegetable, cooking the zucchini and eggplant for 5–7 minutes on each side and the capsicum and onion for 3–5 minutes on each side.

In the same pan, fry the grated tomato for 6–8 minutes, until it begins to darken in colour.

Preheat the oven to 180°C (350°F) fan-forced.

Spoon a layer of the tomato sauce in the base of a large earthenware baking dish and top with half the garlic. Cover with a layer of potato, followed by the zucchini, capsicum, onion and finally the eggplant, seasoning with salt and pepper between each layer. Spoon over the remaining tomato sauce and garlic and tuck the bay leaves in between the vegetables. Drizzle over the honey.

Transfer the dish to the oven and roast for 30 minutes or until you see the juices starting to bubble. Throw the walnuts on top and return to the oven for 10 minutes to toast them slightly.

Serve the vegetables on their own or as part of a spread to accompany whatever you like. This dish goes particularly well with fish, lamb or even a big spoonful of fresh ricotta.

LA ESPINAGADA

Spicy eel and greens pie

SERVES 4–6

'La espinagada' is a free-form family-sized pie from the northern town of Sa Pobla in Mallorca, the only part of the island where eels can be found. The smoked eel in this dish is a great ready-to-use product that gives the taste of the chargrill to help combat the heavy eel fats. Plus it saves a lot of fuss and mess in the kitchen! The addition of chilli is quite rare in Spanish cuisine, but it is used to mask the muddiness of products, such as tripe and, in this case, the slippery eel.

A vegetarian version of this dish is also typically made on the eve of the Fiesta de Sant Antoni (the patron saint of animals), where blessings are made for annual prosperity in agriculture and farming.

1 whole smoked eel (see Note)
6 parsley sprigs, finely chopped
3 garlic cloves, finely chopped
1½ tablespoons extra virgin olive oil
1 lemon, halved
½ teaspoon spicy pimentòn
1 teaspoon sweet pimentòn
4–5 spring onions (scallions), chopped
sea salt flakes and freshly ground black pepper
100 g (3½ oz) silverbeet (Swiss chard) leaves,
    finely chopped

100 g (3½ oz) English spinach leaves,
    finely chopped
1 free-range egg, lightly beaten

Pastry
70 g (2½ oz) lard or butter,
    at room temperature
1 tablespoon extra virgin olive oil
500 g (1 lb 2 oz) plain (all-pupose) flour,
    plus extra for dusting
pinch of fine sea salt

To make the pastry, combine the lard or butter and oil in a large bowl, then slowly add 250 ml (8½ fl oz/1 cup) of water to form a runny paste. Add the flour and salt and use your hands to bring the ingredients together to form a rough dough.

Transfer the dough to a well-floured work surface and briefly knead until the dough comes together. Flatten it with the palm of your hand or a rolling pin into a thick disc, then wrap in plastic wrap and set aside to rest for 30 minutes.

Clean the eel by removing the head and peeling off the skin. Split the eel lengthways and carefully remove all the bones. Cut the eel into eight pieces and transfer to a bowl. Add the parsley, garlic, oil, the juice of one lemon half, both pimentòns and the spring onion. Season to taste, then set aside to marinate for 10 minutes.

Preheat the oven to 180°C (350°F) fan-forced. Line a baking tray with baking paper.

Roll the dough out on a well-floured work surface to a 35 x 20 cm (14¾ x 8 in) rectangle. Transfer to the prepared tray and scatter half the silverbeet and spinach over the dough, leaving a 3–4 cm (1¼–1½ in) border. Spread the marinated eel mixture on top, then cover with the remaining silverbeet and spinach. Brush the borders with a little beaten egg, then fold the two longer sides of dough into the centre to meet in the middle, sealing them together with a few pinches all the way along the top. Fold over each end and pinch to seal.

Make three air holes with a wire skewer or knife along the top of the pie and bake for 40–45 minutes, until golden.

NOTE: You can buy smoked eel from some delicatessens and most fishmongers.

MONGETES EN 'GREVI'

Gravy beans

SERVES 4

Gravy is one of the culinary hangovers from the British occupation of Menorca in the 18th century. It came with the navy and stayed on the plates of locals, and it's still served today with macaroni or fideos and legumes, such as chickpeas (garbanzo beans) or lentils.

There has always been a high consumption of grains and legumes on the islands, and my favourite is the mongeta de careta de Sa Pobla from Mallorca – a beautiful half-white, half kidney bean–coloured round bean that's perfect for a wetter dish like this.

You can use white beans or kidney beans, a mixture of the two or, as I have done here, borlotti beans, especially if you can find some fresh still in their pods. This recipe also uses home-made beef stock to enrich this original island 'baked-bean' experience.

300 g (10½ oz) dried borlotti (cranberry) beans, soaked in cold water overnight, drained
1 rosemary sprig
1 kg (2 lb 3 oz) beef marrowbones, oxtail or knuckle bones
20 g (¾ oz) butter
2 tablespoons extra virgin olive oil
1 field mushroom, roughly chopped
2 onions, roughly chopped
1 carrot, roughly chopped
1 garlic bulb, halved crossways

1 fresh bay leaf
2 tablespoons tomato paste (concentrated purée)
sea salt flakes and freshly ground black pepper
2 litres (2 qts) beef or chicken stock
2 thick English-style, good-quality pork sausages, sliced into rounds
1 marjoram or oregano sprig
1½ tablespoons plain (all-purpose) flour
2 tomatoes, diced
4 poached eggs, to serve (optional)

Place the beans in a large saucepan with the rosemary. Cover with plenty of cold water and bring to the boil. Simmer over medium heat for 40–50 minutes, until the beans are tender. Drain. Remove and discard the rosemary sprig.

Meanwhile, place the beef marrowbones, butter and half the oil in a large stockpot over high heat. Stir the bones to coat in the butter and oil and cook for 10–15 minutes, until they have leached out their juices and turned grey with no blood remaining. Add the mushroom, half the onion, the carrot, garlic, bay leaf and tomato paste and season with salt and pepper. Cook for 10–12 minutes, until the ingredients have turned a dark golden brown. Pour in the stock, bring to the boil, then reduce the heat and gently simmer for 1 hour to let the flavours marry.

Strain the stock into a saucepan and keep warm.

Heat the remaining oil in a large heavy-based frying pan over medium–high heat. Add the sausage and marjoram or oregano and cook for 5 minutes or until the sausage is golden brown. Add the remaining onion and cook for 12–15 minutes, until soft and golden, then add the flour and stir for just under 1 minute to coat the onion. Slowly pour in the stock, stirring to combine, then add the beans. Bring to a simmer, stir through the tomato and cook for 2–3 minutes, until soft.

Serve the gravy beans in bowls for breakfast, lunch or dinner, with a poached egg on top, if you like.

Fishing has always been a fundamental way of life on the Balearics. Some work all year round as commercial fishermen, while for others it's a favourite recreational pastime and a way to enjoy the fruits of the sea at home, or at the many local markets, bars and restaurants.

Although professional fishing is decreasing, its social importance and small-scale practices, handed down through generations, mean that the islands' long relationship with the sea remains culturally important. All around the Balearics you can still find charming old 'casetas' (fishermen's huts) hidden among the rocks and cliffs. Made of stone and sabina wood beams, some of them are home to 'llaüts', traditional wooden fishing boats that are slid along handmade wooden piers from the hut, straight into the sea. However, the beauty of having such diverse coastlines means that a boat is not always needed, and rock and reef fish, cephalopods and sea urchins can be found close to the shore for those who don't want to venture out to sea.

With such a diversity of local seafood, markets and restaurants are always eager to showcase the seasonal catch. Larger fish, such as amberjack, scorpion fish, sea bream, dorado, snapper, grouper, turbot, John dory, flounder and dentex are common, alongside smaller oily fish including anchovies and sardines. Shellfish is also highly prized and prawns (shrimp), lobster, crab, mussels and clams regularly feature in some of the islands' favourite dishes. A simple starter might consist of grilled razor clams, doused in garlic and wine (see page 153), baked scallops topped with local jamón and Mahón cheese (see page 150) and that much-loved 70s classic the prawn cocktail, paired with its sweet salsa rosa and a few melon balls for that extra retro vibe (see page 149).

Although many of the seafood dishes on the islands are unique, the Balearics' culinary relationship with the mainland is never far away. The quintessential Spanish favourite baccalà (salt cod) appears on many menus, often paired with locally grown vegetables, such as artichokes, and coated in a Balearic potato allioli sauce. And, of course, you will always find paella in its many permutations, whether it's fideos in a rich squid-ink sauce or a classic seafood paella served the Balearic way in a silky, soupy broth. This chapter celebrates these classic dishes and if you've visited the Balearic Islands, you will understand the reverence placed on this precious resource and the uniqueness of each dish. If you haven't, then the following pages will show you yet another side to Spain's love for the fruits of the sea.

CÓCTEL DE GAMBES

Prawn cocktail

SERVES 4

The Balearic Islands was the place to be in the 60s and 70s, as the package tourism boom brought holidaymakers in search of paradise and a place to relax and unwind. The upper echelons of British society were drawn here for the beautiful climate and spectacular coastlines, glamourous 'fincas', mega yachts, al fresco dining, parties and an extremely good exchange rate. Luxurious, stylish, fashionable, private and isolated, the Hollywood A-lister jet-set soon caught on and stars including Elizabeth Taylor, Sean Connery, Roger Moore and music legends, such as Lennon, Dylan, Hendrix and Jagger, began visiting the islands to escape the limelight. I can just picture them lounging around, a glass of prawn cocktail with 'salsa rosa' in one hand and a gin and tonic in the other.

16 large cooked prawns (shrimp), peeled and deveined with tails left intact
100 g (3½ oz) finely shredded iceberg lettuce
200 g (7 oz) honeydew melon or rockmelon (canteloupe), balled or cubed
¼ avocado, sliced lengthways
½ orange, thinly sliced
4 small tarragon sprigs

Salsa rosa
80 g (2¾ oz/⅓ cup) mahonesa (see page 125)
2 tablespoons tomato ketchup
juice of ½ orange
2 teaspoons whisky or brandy
pinch of sea salt flakes and white pepper
¼ bunch chives, finely snipped

Combine the salsa rosa ingredients in a small bowl.

Set aside four prawns and roughly chop the remaining twelve prawns into 1 cm (½ in) chunks, discarding the tails. Fold the chopped prawns through the salsa rosa.

Arrange the shredded lettuce in the base of four cocktail, martini or dessert glasses and top with half the chopped prawn mixture. Divide the melon balls among the glasses and spoon the remaining prawn mixture on top. Gently place the avocado and orange slices upright in each glass. Finish with a prawn perched on top and sprinkle over the tarragon.

VIEIRAS AL FORN GRATINADES

Baked scallops

SERVES 4

Baked scallops are traditionally a Galician dish, but they're also enjoyed on special occasions throughout Spain. The majority of Spanish scallops are caught off the Atlantic coast in Galicia, however the Balearics benefit from being the westernmost point of habitation for the wonderful Mediterranean scallop, allowing the islanders to keep this dish truly local.

I leave the roe on but feel free to remove it if you're not a fan.

16 scallops with roe in half shells
3 tablespoons dry white wine
1 garlic clove, minced
2 teaspoons freshly squeezed lemon juice
pinch of sea salt flakes and white pepper
25 g (1 oz) freshly blitzed fine breadcrumbs
4 slices jamón or prosciutto, thinly sliced and finely chopped
2 teaspoons grated Mahón reserva or parmesan
1 teaspoon finely chopped thyme leaves
zest of ¼ lemon, plus lemon wedges to serve
2 tablespoons extra virgin olive oil
pinch of freshly ground black pepper

Preheat the grill (broiler) to medium–high.

Place the scallop shells on a large baking tray.

In a small bowl, combine the white wine, garlic, lemon juice and salt and white pepper. Spoon ½ teaspoon of the mixture into each shell.

Combine the remaining ingredients in a separate bowl, then scatter the mixture over each scallop. Place the scallops under the grill at least 10 cm (4 in) away from the heat and grill for 6–8 minutes, until the scallops have shrunk a little and the crumbs are golden and toasted.

Transfer to a serving platter and serve with lemon wedges on the side.

NAVALLES A LA PLANXA

Grilled razor clams

SERVES 4

Mostly fished off the coast of northwest Spain, these long-shelled fingers of the sea are found on tapas menus all over the country. When I worked in Ibiza a few years ago, I couldn't get enough of these tasty morsels and I'd seek them out with purpose on my days off. My most memorable experience was at the Restaurante El Carmen in Cala d'Hort, sitting alone looking at the enigmatic, isolated island of Es Verdrà, while sucking razor clam shells clean.

If you don't mind an imported frozen product, then do give this dish a try. Otherwise, wait until your next trip to Spain, hit the local seafood market and cook up these sweet-tasting clams for your travelling crew, fresh and simple. Here, I've swapped out the typical parsley picada for island fennel flavours. Delicious!

1 teaspoon fennel seeds
3 garlic cloves, finely chopped
1 tablespoon extra virgin olive oil
80 ml (2½ fl oz/⅓ cup) dry white wine
pinch of sea salt flakes and freshly ground black pepper
24 razor clams in their shells
2 fennel fronds or dill sprigs, fronds picked

Lightly toast the fennel seeds in a small frying pan over medium heat, until they just start to release their oils and begin to hiss in the pan. Transfer to a mortar and pestle and grind to a coarse powder. Place in a bowl with the garlic, half the oil, the wine and salt and pepper.

Heat a large heavy-based, well-seasoned flat griddle plate or gas barbecue hotplate on high until smoking hot. You will need to work in batches so have some paper towel handy to wipe the plate clean between each batch. Brush the plate with a little of the remaining oil and place the clams, hinge side down, on the plate. With tongs at the ready, turn them over as soon as they open and press down on the shells to flatten the flesh against the plate. Cook for 1 minute or until browned, then spoon over some of the dressing. Cover and steam the clams for a few seconds, then transfer to a plate and keep warm while you cook the rest, bringing the heat back up to high and applying another drizzle of oil before adding the next batch.

Drizzle the garlic and juices from the plate over the cooked clams and serve with the fennel or dill fronds scattered over the top.

SARDINES DE ROMANI

Rosemary-skewered sardines

SERVES 4

Butterflying fish is a great way to get rid of all those bones, plus it saves you doing all the work at the other end, which can get in the way of eating. The flattened fish also allows for even grilling, while threading them onto long skewers gives you the perfect instrument with which to flip them over.

Rosemary grows wild all over the Balearic Islands and it's pretty much available all year round. Luckily, the same also goes for my backyard, so I came up with the idea to use rosemary stalks as ready-made skewers to help flavour these fantastic little fish. Just trim a few sturdy stalks into 10 cm (4 in) lengths and pluck off most of the leaves, leaving one end with a few leaves to use as a handle.

20 butterflied sardines, tails attached

20 sturdy rosemary stalks, leaves picked (or use bamboo skewers), soaked in water for 2 hours

sea salt flakes

3 tablespoons extra virgin olive oil

1 teaspoon butter

60 g (2 oz/¾ cup) freshly blitzed fine breadcrumbs

2 garlic cloves, finely chopped

zest of ½ lemon

1 thyme sprig, leaves finely chopped

1 marjoram or oregano sprig, leaves finely chopped

freshly ground black pepper

2 tablespoons sherry vinegar

½ lemon

Tomato jam (see page 60) or your favourite condiment, to serve

Prepare a charcoal grill and wait until the flames have died down and the coals have an even coating of white ash.

Place two sardines on a chopping board with their longest edge facing you. Pierce two skewers through both sides of the sardines, then sprinkle a little salt evenly over the fillets. Repeat with the remaining sardines and set aside for 20 minutes.

Heat 1 tablespoon of the oil and the butter in a frying pan over medium heat. Add the breadcrumbs and garlic and cook, tossing the pan, until the breadcrumbs have absorbed the oil and butter. Add the lemon zest and herbs and cook, swirling the pan to evenly distribute the crumbs, until they are golden and crisp. Set aside on paper towel to absorb any residual oil, then sprinkle with salt and pepper.

When the coals are ready, give the grill a good scrub with a grill brush, then season with a clean rag dabbed in half the remaining oil (be careful it doesn't drip into the fire and flare up).

Pat the fish dry with paper towel, then lightly sprinkle over the sherry vinegar and rub the remaining oil into the sardines. Transfer the sardines to one end of the hot grill and cook for 2–3 minutes, until charred and the sardines lift easily from the grill. Gently flip the fish over and cook for a further 2–3 minutes.

Transfer the skewered sardines to a large platter and squeeze the lemon over the top. Scatter over the toasted breadcrumb mixture and serve with tomato jam or your favourite condiment on the side.

BORRIDA DE BACALLÀ

Cod in bourride

SERVES 4

Menorca belonged to the French for only seven years, but I like to think that this dish is linked to that period in the 18th century, or maybe it's just a simple fisherman's stew that's been passed down from one neighbouring Mediterranean coastline to another.

This hybrid of France's 'other' fish stew from Provence (not the star bouillabaisse), bourride is a delicate and simple fish broth thickened with 'all i oli' (aïoli), meaning garlic and oil. Commonly served with skate over in Ibiza and Formentera, the Menorcans add a boiled potato and a pinch of pimentòn to the salty cod poaching liquid and very little else.

It's important to taste the poaching liquid as you cook it and add more water if it becomes too salty. Also, don't allow the mixture to boil or it will split and you'll have to start again!

4 whole artichokes, stalks trimmed
½ lemon, quartered
1 desiree potato
2 fresh bay leaves
2 thyme sprigs
4 garlic cloves, minced
sea salt flakes

180 ml (6 fl oz) extra virgin olive oil
4 x 170 g (6 oz) baccalà fillets (salt cod), soaked
    in cold water for 24 hours, drained
¼ teaspoon sweet pimentòn
60 g (2 oz) chilled butter, diced
2 parsley sprigs, leaves chopped (optional)
crusty baguette, to serve

Remove the hard outer leaves from the artichokes, then slice off the top one-third and scoop out and discard the fibrous centres using a melon baller or a sharp-edged teaspoon. Peel the outer layer of the stalks, then place the artichokes in a bowl of cold water with the lemon squeezed in.

Place the potato in a saucepan with plenty of salted water and bring to the boil. Cook for 12–15 minutes, until tender, then drain and set aside to cool. When cool enough to handle, peel and grate the potato into a bowl.

Meanwhile, drain the artichokes and place in a separate saucepan with plenty of cold salted water and one of the bay leaves and the thyme. Bring to the boil and cook for 20–30 minutes, until the outer leaves pull away easily from the core. Drain and set aside, discarding the bay leaf and thyme.

Using a mortar and pestle, pound the garlic with a pinch of salt to a fine paste. Add the potato and mix well, then, stirring continuously, gradually add 150 ml (5 fl oz) of the oil until completely incorporated.

Place the baccalà in a deep frying pan and cover with 1.5 litres (51 fl oz/6 cups) of water. Add the remaining bay leaf and pimentòn and gently warm over medium–low heat until just beginning to steam and simmer. Using a slotted spoon, remove the baccalà and transfer to a plate lined with paper towel to drain. Remove 375 ml (12½ fl oz/1½ cups) of the poaching liquid and gradually stir it into the potato allioli.

Heat the remaining oil and half the butter in a heavy-based frying pan over medium heat and add the baccalà. Cook for 3–4 minutes on each side until lightly golden, then reduce the heat to medium–low. Add the potato allioli and artichoke hearts and stir through, making sure the sauce doesn't boil. Once the sauce is heated through, add the remaining butter in three batches and stir until shiny and well combined.

Transfer to a serving dish and scatter over the parsley (if using). Serve with plenty of the sauce and a big crusty baguette on the side.

ANGULA A LA BRASA

Barbecued eel

SERVES 4

'Angula' (baby eels) are a huge delicacy on mainland Spain and at €600 a kilo, one of the most expensive, too. They are hugely popular in the northern provinces where you'll find these tiny, grey-bellied, noodle-like fish on supermarket shelves, along with a modern, cheaper imitation called 'gulas', which are made from the Japanese fish paste surimi. The taste is virtually the same due to the subtle flavour of 'angulas', but you will notice a slight textural difference.

A much more sustainable practice exists over in the village of Sa Pobla in Mallorca, where the famous Espinagada eel pie (see page 141) comes from. There, large bonfires are lit across the island for Sant Antoni (Saint Anthony), who also happens to be the patron saint of this popular little town. These festivities coincide with the local eel season and celebrations in the village also include an entire gastronomic event devoted to this local freshwater fish, where many participating bars and restaurants offer this simple way of preparing eel as an alternative to some of the classic, richer dishes.

2 x 800–900 g (1 lb 12 oz–2 lb) eels, cleaned and gutted, skin on
2 teaspoons fine sea salt
3½ tablespoons extra virgin olive oil
freshly ground black pepper
2 teaspoons sherry vinegar

1½ lemons
3 garlic cloves, finely chopped
4 spring onions (scallions), finely chopped
½ teaspoon spicy pimentòn
½ bunch chives, finely chopped
¼ teaspoon white pepper

Remove the eels' heads just behind the gills. With one eel on its side, carefully slice from the neck down the backbone, running the knife between the flesh and the bones. Detach the fillet, then turn the eel over and remove the other fillet. Repeat with the remaining eel, then cut each fillet into 6.5 cm (2½ in) lengths. Place the fillets in a colander and sprinkle the salt on both sides of the fillets. Set aside for 1 hour.

Meanwhile, prepare a charcoal or hibachi grill and wait until the flames have died down and the coals have an even coating of white ash. You want to achieve a gentle, moderate heat to give the smoke enough time to penetrate the eel.

When the coals are ready, give the grill a good scrub with a grill brush, then season with a clean rag dabbed in a little of the oil (be careful it doesn't drip into the fire and flare up).

Pat the eel fillets dry with paper towel, then season with salt and pepper and rub in 1 tablespoon of the remaining oil.

Transfer to the hot grill and cook for 6–10 minutes, until the eel is charred and lifts easily from the grill. Sprinkle over half the vinegar, then gently flip the eel over and cook for a further 6–10 minutes, until cooked through. Sprinkle with the remaining vinegar just before you pull the eel off the coals. Transfer to a large serving platter.

Slice the ends off the whole lemon. Place one end flat on a chopping board and, using a sharp knife, slice off the peel and white pith. Slice into the lemon either side of each segment and gently pull the segments to release them. Roughly chop the segments, then combine in a small bowl with the juice from the remaining lemon half, the remaining oil, the garlic, spring onion, pimentòn, chives and white pepper.

Cut the eel into sections as big or as small as you like and spoon over the lemon salsa.

MUSCLERES DE MAHONESA

Mahón mussels with mayonnaise

SERVES 4

Menorca has the largest natural harbour in the Mediterranean, and the second largest in the world after Pearl Harbor. The port of Mahón is home to such a diverse array of heritage and stories all coming together to make it a truly unique place. Restaurants, tourists, locals, boats, ferries and a naval base, not to mention a foreign soldiers' cemetery, 19th century fortress and an old quarantine station, all sit side by side in parallel, quietly telling the history of the island. And then there's mussels and mayonnaise, two small and humble ingredients with so much of their own history and culture stemming from this incredibly fascinating and eclectic little hub.

I've added a bit of spice, which you might get offered in the form of hot sauce at some restaurants, as it's a favourite to eat with quality tinned shellfish over there. I also love putting this mix into a sandwich with a bit of lettuce and serving it as an aperitif.

80 ml (2½ fl oz/⅓ cup) dry white wine
1 fresh bay leaf
1.3 kg (2 lb 14 oz) mussels, scrubbed
   and debearded
250 g (9 oz/1 cup) mahonesa (see page 125)
1 garlic clove, minced
½ teaspoon hot English mustard
2 teaspoons freshly squeezed lemon juice

½ bunch chives, finely chopped
2 green chillies, deseeded and finely diced
sea salt flakes and white pepper
shredded lettuce, to serve
hot sauce, to serve
lemon wedges, to serve
sliced sandwich bread, to serve (optional)
sliced gherkin (dill pickle), to serve (optional)

Place the wine, bay leaf and 250 ml (8½ fl oz/1 cup) of water in a large stockpot over high heat. Bring to a simmer, then add the mussels and cook, covered, for 4–6 minutes, until the shells just begin to open. Using a slotted spoon, immediately remove the mussels and set aside in a bowl. Leave any stragglers in there a little longer to see if they'll open and remove when they do. Keep the pan juices simmering until you have about 125 ml (4 fl oz/½ cup) of liquid remaining. Strain into a small bowl to remove any impurities and discard any mussels that haven't opened.

Once the mussels are cool enough to handle, separate the flesh from the shells and place in a non-reactive bowl with the mahonesa, garlic, mustard, lemon juice, chives and green chilli. Season with salt and white pepper and stir to combine.

Serve the mussels as a salad on a bed of shredded lettuce with hot sauce and lemon wedges on the side or in a sandwich with extra hot sauce and a few slices of gherkin.

MAHONES

A

Allegedly invented by a Minorcan, this old-school emulsified cold sauce was said to have been 'taken back' to France by a delighted Duke after the occupation of Menorca in the mid 1700s. Long proclaimed as French in origin, they gave it their name mayonnaise, vulgarised from the original spelling which was taken from the Port of Maó in Mahón (pronounced 'Mayon'), resulting in the name 'mahonesa'.

Indeed it was the French who popularised this sauce throughout Europe and the Americas, and today mayonnaise can be found in every household fridge in the Western world, where it is fondly known as simply 'mayo'. Everybody has their favourite brand they like to use including the Japanese sweeter style 'Kewpie'. Lathered on bread in a sandwich, scooped up with hot chips (fries) or used as a base for dips, dressings and sauces, the uses for this incredibly

versatile mother sauce are seemingly endless. Unfortunately, cheap imitations are rife, along with less-than-satisfactory low-fat, soy, salty, sweet and watery commercial options. When it comes to real mayonnaise, you can't beat the original thick, creamy, stable blend of oil and egg flavoured with your preferred acid of vinegar or lemon juice.

Garlic and mustard are also popular flavour additions with the former 'allioli' (aïoli) proving to be nearly as popular as the original. If you want to diversify your mayonnaise even further, then try adding seaweed, miso, bacon bits or soy sauce to take it into umami territory. Honey, tomato ketchup and liqueurs will sweeten your mayonnaise, while anchovies, capers and herbs will lead to a more savoury experience. Whichever you choose, you will be richly rewarded.

FIDEUA NEGRE

Squid ink fideo paella

SERVES 4

The Catalans lay claim to this dish, but you'll find it all over the Balearic Islands. It's fantastic to share, sitting around the table on a summer's afternoon and rinsing away the black dye left on your lips with a few bottles of 'vino rosado'.

12 large clams or pipis
2½ tablespoons extra virgin olive oil
300 g (10½ oz) fideo pasta or thick spaghetti cut into 2.5 cm (1 in) lengths
2 garlic cloves, smashed
1 red capsicum (bell pepper), finely diced
2 x 150 g (5½ oz) whole calamari, cleaned, hoods finely diced, tentacles set aside
1 onion, finely diced
2 ripe tomatoes, grated, skins discarded
sea salt flakes

125 ml (4 fl oz/½ cup) dry sherry
1 litre (34 fl oz/4 cups) good-quality fish stock, plus extra if needed
4 x 8 g (⅓ oz) squid ink sachets
8 large raw prawns (shrimp), heads removed
lemon wedges, to serve

Allioli
185 g (6½ oz/¾ cup) mahonesa (see page 125) or good-quality whole egg mayonnaise
2 garlic cloves, minced

Preheat the oven to 180°C (350°F) fan-forced.

Place the clams in a large bowl and cover with plenty of cold water. Set aside for 1 hour to purge them of any sand or grit, then drain and set aside.

Meanwhile, toss 2 tablespoons of the oil with the fideos in a large bowl until well coated. Spread the fideos in a single layer on two large baking trays and bake for 6–8 minutes, stirring and rotating the pasta to evenly toast. Remove from the oven and set aside.

Heat the remaining oil in a 32–34 cm (12¾–13½ in) paella pan or large ovenproof frying pan over medium–low heat and add the garlic and capsicum. Gently sauté for 8–10 minutes, until soft and the colour has leached out of the capsicum into the oil. Using a slotted spoon, remove the capsicum from the pan and set aside on a small plate.

Add the diced calamari and sauté for 3–4 minutes, then add the onion and cook for 10–12 minutes, until softened and beginning to colour. Stir in the grated tomato and 1 teaspoon of salt and increase the heat to medium. Cook, stirring frequently, for 12–15 minutes, until you have a chocolate-coloured 'sofrito'. Stir through the sherry and cook until evaporated.

Meanwhile, pour the stock into a saucepan and bring to the boil over high heat. Remove the pan from the heat and stir through the squid ink.

Stir the toasted fideos into the 'sofrito' and mix well to coat. Add the stock and gently shake the pan to evenly distribute the pasta, then reduce the heat to low and simmer for 10 minutes or until the liquid has evaporated. If you're unable to achieve an even heat, rotate the pan around the burners on the stovetop, so that each side of the pan cooks evenly.

Place the clams, prawns and calamari tentacles on top of the fideos and continue to cook, shaking the pan occasionally, for 4–5 minutes. If you don't trust the surface of your pan, create a few holes in the mixture using the end of a wooden spoon to check if the base is burning. If so, reduce the heat to the lowest setting and add a little more stock if necessary. Scatter the reserved capsicum over the top and transfer the pan to the oven for 10 minutes.

To make the allioli, combine the mahonesa and garlic in a small bowl with a pinch of salt.

Serve the paella in the centre of the table with lemon wedges and the allioli on the side.

POPS ESTOFATS

Stewed baby octopus

SERVES 4

Octopus features in several Balearic dishes, from chargrilled with potatoes or deep-fried baby octopus, to salads and this heartier, wintery, one-dish wonder.

Octopus grow very fast, daily. They're made up of 80–90 per cent water, which is why it's always recommended to freeze them as part of the tenderising process. Or more often than not, you will buy them already frozen. When frozen, the water expands and penetrates the the proteins as the octopus defrosts. The long cooking time in this recipe also helps this tenderising process, which results in a sweet and gentle flavour.

2 teaspoons black peppercorns
1 kg (2 lb 3 oz) baby octopus
fine sea salt
60 ml (2 fl oz/¼ cup) extra virgin olive oil
1 fresh bay leaf
80 ml (2½ fl oz/⅓ cup) brandy
50 g (1¾ oz) butter
3 onions, sliced
1 star anise
125 ml (4 fl oz/½ cup) dry white wine
125 ml (4 fl oz/½ cup) passata (puréed tomatoes)
1 teaspoon sweet pimentòn
3 garlic cloves, sliced
150 ml (5 fl oz) good-quality fish stock or water

Coarsely crush the peppercorns using a mortar and pestle and set aside.

Submerge the baby octopus in 2 litres (2 qts) of water mixed with 2 teaspoons of salt, and set aside for 15 minutes. Drain.

Heat half the oil in a large frying pan over high heat until very hot. Working in batches and taking care not to let the octopus ignite, cook the octopus for 4 minutes, then remove from the pan using a slotted spoon. Add the final batch of octopus, the bay leaf, the ground peppercorns and brandy and sauté for 4 minutes or until the alcohol has evaporated. Remove from the pan and add to the rest of the octopus.

Meanwhile, heat the remaining oil and the butter in a separate frying pan over medium heat. Add the onion with a pinch of salt and sauté for 5 minutes. Stir through the star anise and white wine, then cover and cook for 10 minutes or until the onion is soft. Remove the lid once the liquid has evaporated, then stir through the passata and pimentòn for 5 minutes. Add the sautéed octopus and stir to combine, then add the garlic and stock or water, bring to a simmer, cover and cook for 15 minutes or until reduced.

This dish is best cooled to room temperature and then left overnight in the fridge to really bring the flavours together (there's something about the gelatine in the octopus that relaxes and leaches into the sauce, so you really notice the difference), but if you're short on time, you can let it cool for 2 hours before reheating and serving.

PEIX DE ROCA EN SALSA ANXOA

Rockfish in anchovy sauce

SERVES 4

Rockfish is the generic name given to several popular species of fish in the Mediterranean. Snorkelling off local coastlines, you can easily spot these beautiful-coloured fish feeding away between the rocks and burrowing in the sand when you get too close. Little razor fish, red mullet and scorpion fish are among the favourites frequently added to soups, stocks or broths or used in stews or fried. Here I've used red mullet, which is more readily available.

I like to serve these little guys fried whole, but you can remove the heads if you like for a daintier audience. Keep the tails on though! They're good to use as a handle, have a great colour and crisp up well when fried. Red mullet are quite small, making them an ideal appetiser, or double the recipe for a larger meal and serve it with your favourite cooked potatoes. To me, the salty, sharp hit of the anchovy sauce perfectly sums up the flavour of the Balearic Islands and it takes me back there again and again.

4 x 150 g (5½ oz) whole red mullet,
    gutted and cleaned
juice of 1 lemon
2 teaspoons sea salt flakes
½ bunch of parsley, leaves picked
2 French shallots, thinly sliced
35 g (1¼ oz/¼ cup) plain (all-purpose) flour
2 free-range eggs, lightly beaten
15 g (½ oz/¼ cup) panko breadcrumbs

25 g (1 oz/¼ cup) dried breadcrumbs
freshly ground black pepper
60 ml (2 fl oz/¼ cup) extra virgin olive oil
100 g (3½ oz) butter
8 anchovy fillets, drained
3 garlic cloves, minced
125 ml (4 fl oz/½ cup) dry white wine
50 ml (1¾ fl oz) good-quality fish stock or water
¼ teaspoon sweet pimentòn

Pat the fish dry with paper towel, then rub over half the lemon juice and the salt, including inside the cavities. Set aside for 15 minutes.

Meanwhile, combine the parsley and shallot in a small bowl and set aside.

Place the flour in a shallow bowl, the beaten egg in another shallow bowl and both breadcrumbs in a third. Grab each fish by its tail and pass it through the plain flour and the beaten egg, then evenly coat in the breadcrumbs. Crack some black pepper over the top of each crumbed fish.

Heat the oil in a large frying pan over medium–high heat. When the oil is hot (test it by throwing in a breadcrumb and waiting for it to sizzle), add two of the fish and fry on both sides for 3–5 minutes, until golden and crisp. Set aside on a tray lined with paper towel and and keep warm while you cook the remaining fish.

Melt the butter in a small saucepan over medium heat and stir through the anchovies, mashing them with a fork as they sizzle. Stir through the garlic for 30 seconds, then pour in half the remaining lemon juice, the white wine and stock or water. Cook for 3–5 minutes, until the sauce has reduced and thickened slightly, then remove from the heat and stir through the remaining lemon juice.

Serve the fish with a good spoonful of anchovy sauce, a little parsley and shallot and a sprinkling of pimentòn.

PEIX A LA BRASA

Chargrilled whole fish

SERVES 4

With so many wonderful beach-shack eateries on the islands, there's no better way to eat whole fish, straight from the makeshift outdoor chargrill and onto your plate after an afternoon swim. Sun, beach, sangria and grilled fish. Repeat. That's what summertime on the Balearic Islands means.

So simple, yet not so easy to get right, the locals know their grilled fish. They send their fish 'back to the sea' by submerging them in a brine slurry before cooking. Apart from helping to season the fish from the outside in, this process also partially sets the proteins close to the surface of the skin, which prevents the fish from drying out and sticking when placed on the grill.

200 g (7 oz) fine sea salt
2 x 800 g (1 lb 12 oz) whole snapper, bream or
    sea bass, cleaned and gutted, scales left on
3 tablespoons sherry vinegar
25 g (1 oz) raisins
1 bunch silverbeet (Swiss chard),
    stalks removed

25 g (1 oz) pine nuts
1 small onion, finely diced
3 garlic cloves, thinly sliced
⅓ teaspoon ground cinnamon
pinch of freshly ground black pepper
3 tablespoons extra virgin olive oil
lemon wedges, to serve

Make a slurry with the salt and 500 ml (17 fl oz/2 cups) of water in a large non-reactive dish. Rub the fish all over with the salt water, as well as inside the cavity, then set aside at room temperature for 1 hour.

Prepare a charcoal grill for grilling in two zones. Keep one end burning quite intensely and the other end with a more moderate heat. Wait until the flames have died down and the coals have an even coating of white ash.

Meanwhile, bring the sherry vinegar and raisins to the boil in a small saucepan over medium heat, then remove from the heat and set aside.

Finely shred the silverbeet leaves and place in a large bowl with the pine nuts, onion, garlic, cinnamon, pepper and 2 teaspoons of the oil. Mix well to combine, then add the raisins and 2 teaspoons of the soaking vinegar.

Using paper towel, wipe the salt water from the fish until completely dry. Set aside for a further 15 minutes at room temperature to continue to air-dry.

Stuff the silverbeet mixture inside the cavities of both fish.

When the coals are ready, give the grill a good scrub with a grill brush, then season with a clean rag dabbed in a little of the oil (be careful it doesn't drip into the fire and flare up).

Rub the fish well with the remaining oil and gently place at the hot end of the grill. Cook for 6–10 minutes, until charred and the fish lifts easily from the grill. Gently flip the fish over and cook the other side for a further 6–10 minutes until charred and cooked through. If the fish is still a little pink inside, but charred on the skin, transfer the fish to the cooler end of the grill to finish cooking.

Serve with lemon wedges and enjoy the crispy skin!

ARRÒS A BANDA

Rice on the side

SERVES 4

Originating from Alicante, 'a banda', meaning 'apart', is a fisherman's paella simply made using the leftovers from the daily catch, boiled up into a stock, along with a few pieces of fish reserved for the top of the paella.

Over on Formentera and Ibiza, this traditional favourite is usually served with the fish on the side (hence its name) in the form of the fish stew 'bullit de peix' (see opposite). I also like to serve it this way, but this rice dish is equally satisfying on its own with a chunky garden salad. Always, always serve with more allioli than you think you'll need, and if you're considering serving both dishes, make a double batch and reserve half of it for the bullit sauce.

2 tablespoons extra virgin olive oil
1 onion, finely chopped
2 garlic cloves, finely chopped
pinch of sea salt flakes
150 g (5½ oz) calamari hoods, cleaned and
  finely minced
200 g (7 oz) small peeled raw prawns (shrimp)
2 large tomatoes, grated, skins discarded
2 teaspoons sweet pimentòn
250 ml (8½ fl oz/1 cup) white wine
200 g (7 oz) short-grain rice, such as
  bomba or calasparra
freshly ground black pepper

1 litre (34 fl oz/4 cups) Ibizan fish stew fish
  stock (see opposite) or store-bought
  fish stock, heated to a simmer,
  plus extra if needed
pinch of saffron
lemon wedges, to serve

Allioli
2 free-range egg yolks
3 garlic cloves, peeled
sea salt flakes
250 ml (8½ fl oz/1 cup) extra virgin olive oil

To make the allioli, blitz the egg yolks, peeled garlic and a big pinch of salt flakes in the small bowl of a food processor or in a jug using a hand-held blender, until combined to a paste. With the motor running, slowly add the oil, one drop at a time at first and then gradually drizzling in a thin, steady stream, until you have a thick mayonnaise. Transfer to a serving jug and set aside.

Heat the oil in a large 32–34 cm (12¾–13½ in) paella pan or frying pan over medium heat. Add the onion, garlic and a pinch of salt and sauté for 12–15 minutes, until soft. Stir through the calamari and cook for 3–4 minutes, until starting to turn golden. Add the prawns and stir through, then add the grated tomato and pimentòn and cook for a further 5 minutes or until you have a deep-coloured, thick paste. Pour in the wine and cook until completely evaporated, then add the rice and stir well to coat the grains. Season with black pepper.

Add three-quarters of the stock and the saffron, and keep stirring until the mixture comes to the boil. Reduce the heat to medium–low and gently simmer for 12–15 minutes, until most of the liquid has evaporated. If you're unable to achieve an even heat, rotate the pan around the burners on the stovetop, so that each side of the pan cooks evenly. Pour in the remaining stock, then gently shake the pan from side to side to distribute the liquid. If you don't trust the surface of your pan, create a few holes in the mixture using the end of a wooden spoon or spatula to check if the base is burning. If so, reduce the heat to the lowest possible setting and add a little more stock if the pan is very dry. Continue to simmer over low heat for a further 6–8 minutes, until the rice is cooked through.

Remove from the heat and serve immediately in bowls with the allioli and lemon wedges on the side and the fish stew opposite, if you're game.

BULLIT DE PEIX

Ibizan fish stew

SERVES 4

Bullit de peix is the epitomy of Ibizan gastronomy, and it's likely to be the first dish a local recommends you to try. Translated as 'boiled fish', it's served in two parts, so you want to make a day of it, which is usually Sunday for the locals. First up, great-quality fish is poached (with or without potatoes, contentiously) and then served with a rich allioli. The stock is then used to cook 'arròs a banda' (see opposite) for the second course. This crunchy-bottomed, exquisitely simple rice is one of the best things I've ever eaten. On my first Sunday on the island, I was taken to Restaurante Port Balansat on the beach at Port Sant Miquel in the north and sat down to this decadent, bright yellow platter of fish in a little stock. I thought, how are we going to get through all of this magnificent fish? And then came the rice! Sure enough, after a few bottles of white wine I couldn't stop myself.

If you like, you can add potato and forget about the rice, or do as the locals do and feast your Sunday away in gluttony.

2 x 300 g (10½ oz) whole fish, such as rock fish, red emperor, monkfish, rock ling, red snapper or leather jacket, cleaned and gutted, tails and fins intact
4 x 160 g (5½ oz) fish cutlets, such as trevally, hake or king fish
100 g (3½ oz) fine sea salt
freshly ground black pepper
2 tablespoons extra virgin olive oil
1 onion finely diced
2 garlic cloves, minced
sea salt flakes
2 tomatoes, grated, skins discarded

1 green capsicum (bell pepper), cut into 8 chunks
250 ml (8½ fl oz/1 cup) dry white wine
2 pinches of saffron
3 litres (3 qts) good-quality fish stock, heated to a simmer
4 potatoes, peeled and halved
4 raw scampi
300 g (10½ oz) Roman or flat (runner) beans, trimmed and halved
1 x quantity Allioli (see opposite), plus extra to serve
2 lemons, halved

Remove the heads from the whole fish and cut the fish in half crossways.

Salt the fish cutlets and fish with the fine sea salt and some black pepper and set aside in a large colander in the sink for 30 minutes.

Heat the oil in a large saucepan over medium heat. Add the onion, garlic and a pinch of salt flakes and cook for 15 minutes or until soft and cooked down to a paste. Add the tomato and cook for 6–8 minutes, until incorporated and broken down, then add the capsicum and stir for 1 minute. Pour in the white wine and add the saffron, fish stock and potato, then bring to a simmer and cook for 8–10 minutes, until slightly reduced. One by one, add the fish and scampi, then reduce the heat to low and simmer for 5 minutes. Add the green beans and cook for a further 4–5 minutes, until the fish is firm and the potato is cooked through. Using a large slotted spoon, gently transfer the fish, scampi, potato, beans and capsicum to a large serving platter. Cover with foil and keep warm while you finish the sauce.

Strain 500 ml (17 fl oz/2 cups) of the fish stock into a large jug and strain the remaining stock into a container to use for the second course, 'arròs a banda'.

Once the stock in the jug has cooled a little, add 2 tablespoons to the allioli and whisk to combine. Continue to add the liquid in this way until you reach a cream consistency.

Spoon the sauce over the fish and vegetables and serve with the lemon halves and allioli.

Rice on the side

Ibizan fish stew

PARGO AMB TOMÀTIGA

Red snapper and tomato salad

SERVES 4

There are many Mediterranean dishes that combine seafood and tomatoes, and in this recipe these best friends come together to make a light, restaurant-quality meal that's fresh, light and thoroughly delicious. Sometimes the simple things are the best!

Other sustainable fish, such as sea bass, bream or even barramundi, are also great in this dish.

200 g (7 oz) oxheart or other large heirloom tomatoes, sliced 2 cm (¾ in) thick
200 g (7 oz) vine-ripened tomatoes, sliced 2 cm (¾ in) thick
2 teaspoons sea salt flakes
1 garlic clove, thinly sliced
1 x 650 g (1 lb 7 oz) snapper fillet, skin on
2 tablespoons extra virgin olive oil
1½ tablespoons sherry vinegar
40 g (1½ oz/⅓ cup) pitted black olives
½ celery heart, thinly sliced, leaves reserved
freshly ground black pepper
2 limes, halved, to serve

Place the tomatoes in a bowl and sprinkle over half the salt. Mix through the garlic and set aside to macerate for 20 minutes.

Sprinkle the fish with the remaining salt and set aside in a large colander in the sink for 30 minutes.

Wipe the salt off the fish using paper towel and pat dry as much as you can. Set aside for a further 10 minutes, skin side up, to air-dry some more.

Meanwhile, finish the salad by combining half the oil, the vinegar, olives and celery with the tomatoes.

Heat a large frying pan over high heat. Rub the fish well with the remaining oil and gently place, skin side down, in the pan. Place a piece of baking paper, followed by a weight such as small frying pan, on top of the fish to press the skin flush against the hot pan. Cook for 2–3 minutes, then use a spatula to gently lift a corner of the fish to check that it's not burning (reduce the heat if it is). Keep checking the underside of the fish until it is evenly golden, then flip over and cook for a further 2–3 minutes, depending on the thickness of your fish. You don't want to compress this side, as you may jeopardise the crispness of the skin.

Serve the fish with the tomato salad, a sprinkle of salt flakes and black pepper and the lime halves on the side.

GALL DE SANT PERE

Baked John dory in a caper lemon sauce

SERVES 4

One of the larger catches on the Pitiusas Islands of Ibiza and Formentera is the versatile John dory (known in Spanish as 'gallo de San Pedro', but 'gallo de Sant Pere' in Catalan). A semi-oily fish, it has a sweet, intense flavour, gelatinous skin and a meaty, forgiving texture, making it suitable for many island dishes, whether they're stewed, grilled, baked or fried.

The large spot on the John dory, along with its funky Jurassic-looking head make it a fantastic specimen to display whole, and I love watching people's reactions when I serve this up at the table.

100 g (3½ oz) fine sea salt
1.4 kg (3 lb 1 oz) John dory, gutted and cleaned
1 lemon, thinly sliced
3 thyme sprigs
4 garlic cloves, smashed
1½ tablespoons extra virgin olive oil
50 g (1¾ oz) cold butter, cubed
35 g (1¼ oz) Pickled capers (see page 67) or store-bought capers, drained and rinsed
juice of 2 lemons
sea salt flakes and freshly ground black pepper
Pickled sea fennel (see page 70) or dill or fennel fronds, to serve

Preheat the oven to 220°C (430°F) fan-forced. Line a large baking tray with baking paper.

Rub the salt all over the fish, including inside the cavity. Set aside for 30 minutes.

Wipe the salt off the fish using paper towel and pat dry as much as you can. Set aside for a further 15 minutes to air-dry some more. Keep dabbing the fish with paper towel if liquid continues to leach out.

Stuff the fish cavity with half the lemon, the thyme sprigs and garlic and transfer to the prepared tray. Score the fish a few times, including a vertical slit from the head to the tail.

Evenly rub the oil on both sides of the fish, then transfer to the oven and bake for 15–20 minutes, until golden and cooked through. Allow the fish to rest, loosely covered, while you make the sauce.

Heat half the butter in a frying pan over medium–high heat. Crush the capers with the flat side of a knife and add them to the pan when the butter begins to foam. Sauté for 3–4 minutes, until the capers begin to fry and crisp, then stir through the remaining lemon slices for 1 minute and add the lemon juice. Cook until the liquid has reduced by one-third, then season with salt and pepper. Remove from the heat and stir in the remaining butter, swirling the pan until the butter is completely melted and the sauce is thick and shiny. Fold through the sea fennel, dill or fennel fronds and spoon a few tablespoons of the sauce over the fish.

Serve the fish with an abundance of extra sauce on the side and your favourite side salad.

MANDONGUILLES DE PEIX

Island fish croquettes

SERVES 4

Traditionally, Balearic Island life dictated that no food was wasted. On the island of Formentera, a very old culinary tradition of sun-drying fish still exists today, and you'll often see clotheslines full of hanging butterflied cartilaginous fish, such as stingrays or dogfish. Once dried, they are lightly roasted and pulled apart into strips to conserve in olive oil for the months ahead. Adopting this approach of using up ingredients, I would often make these fish croquettes for staff meals with baccalà fish trimmings, prawn (shrimp) meat and occasionally mussels – basically anything left over that needed using up.

450 g (1 lb) baccalà (salt cod) fillets, soaked
   in cold water for 24 hours, drained
1 white onion, thinly sliced
2 fresh bay leaves
100 g (3½ oz) stale bread, crusts removed
250 ml (8½ fl oz/1 cup) full-cream (whole) milk
1 garlic clove, minced
1 free-range egg
sea salt flakes and freshly ground black pepper
200 g (7 oz) small peeled cooked prawns
   (shrimp), roughly chopped

2 parsley sprigs, leaves chopped
plain (all-purpose) flour, for dusting
2 tablespoons olive oil
2 thyme sprigs
½ small fennel bulb, thinly sliced,
   fronds reserved
2 teaspoons butter
60 ml (2 fl oz/¼ cup) dry white wine or sherry
125 ml (4 fl oz/½ cup) pouring
   (single/light) cream
crusty baguette, to serve (optional)

Place the drained baccalà, onion and bay leaves in a deep frying pan and cover with 1 litre (34 fl oz/4 cups) of water. Gently bring to the boil over medium–low heat, then remove from the heat and set aside to poach for 10 minutes.

Meanwhile, soak the bread in the milk in a small bowl.

Using a slotted spoon, remove the baccalà and onion from the poaching liquid and transfer to a plate lined with paper towel to absorb any excess water. Strain 500 ml (17 fl oz/2 cups) of the poaching liquid into a bowl and set aside. Discard the bay leaves.

Discard any skin or bones from the baccalà and roughly chop into 5 mm (¼ in) pieces. Squeeze the milk from the bread, then transfer the bread (discarding the milk) to the bowl of a food processor, along with the baccalà, garlic and egg. Blitz until well combined, then transfer to a bowl, season with salt and pepper and fold through the prawn and parsley.

With floured hands, divide the mixture into 20 croquettes. Dust the croquettes in flour to coat and set aside.

Preheat the oven to 150°C (300°F) fan-forced. Line a baking tray with baking paper.

Heat 1½ tablespoons of the oil in a deep frying pan and, working in batches, cook the croquettes over high heat for 2–3 minutes on each side until golden. Set aside on paper towel to drain, then transfer to the prepared tray and place in the oven for 6–8 minutes.

Reduce the heat to medium and add the thyme, fennel, butter and remaining oil. Cook for 2 minutes or until the fennel starts to soften, then add 1½ tablespoons of the dusting flour and cook, stirring, for 1 minute. Add the wine and simmer until reduced, then add the reserved poaching liquid and bring to the boil. Reduce the heat to low and stir through the cream and fennel fronds for 2–3 minutes, until the sauce is hot but not simmering.

Transfer the croquettes to shallow serving bowls and spoon over the sauce. Serve with a crusty baguette, if you like.

SÍPIA AMB PÈSOLS

Cuttlefish with peas

SERVES 4

Cuttlefish is a spring catch with a mild and subtle flavour compared to its cephalopod relatives. Underrated in Western cooking, it's seen as very messy and difficult to handle due to its large ink sac and brown, slimy skin. But cooked low and slow, as it is here, the thick flesh melts in your mouth like a semi-cured Mahón cheese, making it worth the effort.

Cuttlefish with peas is a much-loved Mediterranean dish that's also found in Italy and on the mainland peninsula in the Maresme region, where it's common to find seafood paired with something seasonal from the vegetable patch. They will often serve this dish with meatballs and potatoes, too.

700 g (1 lb 9 oz) cuttlefish, squid or calamari hoods, cleaned and cut into 4 cm (1½ in) pieces
2 teaspoons fine sea salt
1½ tablespoons extra virgin olive oil
100 g (3½ oz) pancetta, finely diced
1 white onion, roughly chopped
2 garlic cloves, smashed
sea salt flakes and freshly ground black pepper
1 teaspoon sweet pimentòn
125 ml (4 fl oz/½ cup) dry white wine
3 tomatoes, grated, skins discarded
375 ml (12½ fl oz/1½ cups) good-quality fish stock, plus extra if needed
300 g (10½ oz) fresh or frozen peas
parsley leaves, to serve
crusty bread or boiled potatoes, to serve (optional)
lemon wedges, to serve (optional)

Place the cuttlefish, squid or calamari in a large bowl and cover with plenty of cold water. Stir through half the salt and set aside for 30 minutes. Drain and pat dry with paper towel. Set aside.

Heat the oil in a large frying pan over medium heat and add the pancetta, onion and garlic, along with a pinch of salt and pepper. Gently sauté for 10–15 minutes, until the onion is soft and lightly coloured. Stir through the pimentòn, then add the wine and cook until evaporated. Increase the heat slightly, add the tomato and simmer quite vigorously until the tomato and onion have reduced to a paste. Stir through the cuttlefish and cook until it turns opaque, then pour in the fish stock, reduce the heat and partially cover with a lid. Simmer gently for 40–50 minutes, until the cuttlefish is extremely soft and tender. If the cuttlefish still has some resistance, add a little more stock and continue to cook until soft.

Check the seasoning and adjust if necessary, then add the peas and cook, uncovered, for 15 minutes if using fresh peas or 8 minutes if using frozen.

Divide the cuttlefish and peas among plates and top with a few parsley leaves. Serve with chunks of crusty bread or boiled potatoes and lemon wedges on the side, if you like.

ARRÒS CALDÓS DE MARISC

Seafood paella broth

SERVES 4

Many cultures have a comforting, soupy rice dish to adore and Spain is no exception. The quality of the fish stock is important in this dish, which makes this recipe slightly epic to make, but completely worth it. It's usually served with lobster, but only during spring and summer (due to catchment restrictions); however, you will find this sophisticated seafood paella all year round at restaurants that have frozen some of the season's catch.

2 tablespoons extra virgin olive oil
1 red capsicum (bell pepper), finely diced
300 g (10½ oz) firm white fish fillets, such as
    rock ling, cut into 2–3 cm (¾–1¼ in) chunks
1 onion, finely chopped
2 garlic cloves, minced
sea salt flakes
3 large tomatoes, grated, skins discarded
1 teaspoon smoked pimentòn
100 g (3½ oz) calamari hoods, cleaned
    and diced
400 g (14 oz) short-grain rice, such as bomba
    or calasparra
8 mussels, scrubbed and debearded
4 raw scampi
8 large raw prawns (shrimp), heads and shells
    reserved for the fish stock
2 lemons, halved, to serve

Fish stock
1.5 kg (3 lb 5 oz) large fish heads, bones, fins
    and tails from monkfish, cod or snapper
2 teaspoons olive oil
1 onion, chopped into 8 chunks
1 carrot, chopped into 3 cm (1¼ in) chunks
1 tablespoon tomato paste (concentrated purée)
8 large prawn (shrimp) heads and shells
1 tablespoon fine sea salt
2 fennel stalks, roughly chopped
1 large tomato, roughly chopped
1 fresh bay leaf
8 white peppercorns
60 ml (2 fl oz/¼ cup) dry white wine
3 parsley sprigs
1 pinch of saffron
2.5 litres (2.5 qts) vegetable stock or water

To make the fish stock, rinse the fish heads, bones, fins and tails under cold running water and remove any blood from the larger spinal bones.

Heat the oil in a large stockpot over high heat and add the onion and carrot. Sauté until starting to colour, then add the tomato paste and prawn heads and shells. When the prawn shells begin to toast, add the remaining stock ingredients, including the cleaned fish carcasses and bring to the boil. Reduce the heat to a gentle simmer and skim off any impurities that rise to the surface. Simmer for 35–40 minutes, until reduced by one-third, then remove from the heat and allow to steep for 15 minutes. Strain the stock through a fine-mesh sieve and set aside in a saucepan over low heat.

Heat the oil in a 32–34 cm (12¾–13½ in) paella pan or large frying pan over medium heat. Add the capsicum and sauté for 8–10 minutes, until soft and the colour has leached out into the oil. Remove the capsicum from the pan and set aside. Add the fish fillets to the pan and cook for 3 minutes on both sides until golden. Remove from the pan and set aside. Add the onion and garlic with a pinch of salt and cook for 8–10 minutes, until completely soft. Add the tomato and pimentòn, then reduce the heat to medium–low and cook, stirring frequently, for 15–20 minutes, until the liquid has all but evaporated. Add the calamari and cook for 5 minutes, then add the rice and stir to coat the grains. Pour in three-quarters of the stock and stir until the mixture comes to the boil. Gently simmer for 10–15 minutes, until the rice is cooked through. Pour in the remaining stock, bring to the boil, then add the mussels, scampi, reserved fish fillets, capsicum and prawns. Reduce the heat to a gentle simmer and cook for 5 minutes or until the prawns are cooked through and the mussels have opened. Serve the paella in the pan with the lemon halves for squeezing over.

CALDERETA DE LLANGOSTA

Lobster and gin hotpot

SERVES 4

The sweet-tasting blue spiny lobster is the well-known star of this renowned Menorcan stew fit for kings. Like so many seafood dishes of the Mediterranean, this recipe relies on the care taken and quality of its ingredients, from the 'sofrito' and the stock to the lobster itself. It was once seen as simple sustenance for local fishermen, but now, of course, you have to dig a little deeper into your pockets to enjoy this ultimate taste of the Balearic Islands. Save it for a special occasion – you'll remember it for life and will soon forget what it may have cost you.

If you can manage to get your hands on fresh lobster, make a fast, concise incision at the top of the neck and cut down to slice the head in half lengthways. This protects the meat from tightening and kills the lobster instantly.

2 x 800 g–1 kg (1 lb 12 oz–2 lb 3 oz) live or
    cooked lobsters
1 tablespoon extra virgin olive oil
1 onion, finely diced
4 garlic cloves, finely chopped
sea salt flakes
½ small red capsicum (bell pepper), finely diced
½ small green capsicum (bell pepper),
    finely diced
3 tomatoes, grated, skins discarded
½ teaspoon sweet pimentòn
80 ml (2¾ fl oz/⅓ cup) good-quality gin

2 litres (2 qts) good-quality fish stock
freshly ground black pepper

Picada
200 g (7 oz) stale bread, cut into small chunks
2 tablespoons extra virgin olive oil
1 garlic clove, peeled
pinch of sea salt flakes
35 g (1¼ oz) blanched almonds
pinch of saffron
2 tablespoons brandy
zest of ¼ lemon
juice of ½ lemon

If using live lobsters, use a very sharp knife to make a concise incision at the top of the neck and cut down through the head, cutting it in two. Twist and pull the head from the lobster and pull off the claws. Using a large serrated knife, cut the body crossways into 3–4 cm (1¼–1½ in) medallions. If using cooked lobster, remove the head and cut it in half lengthways, then continue to section the lobster as described above.

Heat the oil in a large frying pan over medium–low heat. Add the onion, garlic and a pinch of salt and gently sauté for 15 minutes or until the onion is completely soft. Add the capsicums and stir, then add the tomato and pimentòn. Cook, stirring frequently, for 20–25 minutes, until the liquid has all but evaporated and the tomato, onion and capsicum have reduced to a paste. Add the lobster heads, cut side down, and pour in the gin. Simmer until the gin has evaporated, then pour in the stock and simmer for 15 minutes or until reduced by one-third.

Meanwhile, to make the picada, toast the bread in a frying pan with the oil over medium heat for 4–6 minutes, until crisp.

Crush the garlic and salt using a mortar and pestle, then pound in the almonds, saffron and toasted bread. Set aside in a serving bowl.

Continue to cook the sauce until it has reduced by half, then add the remaining lobster and continue to simmer for 5–7 minutes, until the lobster is cooked or heated through if using cooked lobster.

Remove from the heat and serve immediately garnished with plenty of black pepper and the picada on the side for spooning over.

GREIXERA DE PEIX A LA MALLORQUINA

Mallorcan-style baked fish

SERVES 6

In this Mallorcan one-dish wonder, freshly cooked fish fillets lie blanketed between delicate potato, spinach and tomato and sprinkled with pine nuts and raisins, to give the dish a true island flavour. Whole fish are also sometimes used and I like to think the tomatoes on top were originally placed to mark the location of the fish underneath, so when it came to serving, everyone would get their portion of fish in one piece. I like to add lots of tomato, as I find the liquid soaks right down to the potatoes, helping to keep the dish moist. It might not be so easy to locate the fish, though!

60 ml (2 fl oz/¼ cup) extra virgin olive oil
500 g (1 lb 2 oz) desiree potatoes, peeled, thinly sliced
2 teaspoons fine sea salt
1 teaspoon sweet pimentòn
1 bunch English spinach, thick stems discarded, roughly chopped
1 bunch spring onions (scallions), sliced
1 bunch parsley, roughly chopped
3 garlic cloves, finely chopped

½ teaspoon ground cinnamon
freshly ground black pepper
6 x 150 g (5½ oz) white fish fillets, such as snapper or flathead
30 g (1 oz) pine nuts
50 g (1¾ oz) raisins
3–4 ripe heirloom tomatoes, sliced
125 ml (4 fl oz/½ cup) dry white wine
lemon wedges, to serve (optional)

Preheat the oven to 180°C (350°F) fan-forced.

Pour 2 tablespoons of the oil into a large earthenware dish or baking dish and layer the potato slices on top. Sprinkle with ½ teaspoon of the fine sea salt and the pimentòn.

In a large colander over a bowl, sprinkle 1 teaspoon of the remaining salt over the spinach and set aside for 20 minutes. Squeeze out as much liquid as possible from the spinach, then transfer to a large bowl and add the spring onion, parsley, garlic and cinnamon. Toss to combine, then spread half the spinach mixture over the potato and press down with your hands to flatten the layers.

Sprinkle the remaining salt and a little pepper over both sides of the fish fillets and place on top of the spinach layer. Top with the remaining spinach mixture, sprinkle over the pine nuts and raisins and finish with the tomato. Pour over the wine and drizzle with the remaining olive oil, then season again with salt and pepper.

Make a cartouche by cutting a circle of baking paper 2 cm (¾ in) wider than your dish. Tuck it into the dish to create a loose seal. Bake on the middle shelf in the oven for 20 minutes, then remove the cartouche and continue to cook for a further 30–40 minutes, until the tomato begins to colour and the potato is cooked through.

Divide into portions, trying to remember where each fish fillet is, and serve with lemon wedges on the side, if you like.

SEA

ith the abundance of seafood surrounding the Balearic Islands, you could be forgiven for thinking the local diet relies solely on what comes from the sea, but head inland to the 'muntanya' or mountain regions and you'll discover another side to Balearic cuisine.

A dedication to preserving traditional agricultural landscapes and practices has contributed to the rise in rural tourism on the islands, away from the package hotel visitors who spend their time basking by the coast. It is here that you'll find a countryside filled with lush pine forests and woodlands of evergreen carob trees. In spring, blossoms of almond and olive trees blanket the fertile land and you'll spot locals foraging for wild mushrooms, fennel and asparagus, which grow freely at the side of the road, ready to pick up and add to the pot for the evening meal.

Dairy is important and cows are abundant in Menorca where their milk is used to make the famous 'Mahón' cheese. Over in Mallorca, pig breeding is still alive and well where the protected indigenous black pig is emblematic to the provincial scenery and production of the prized 'sobrassada' sausage (see page 216). The 'matança' – an ancestral yearly pig slaughter – is still an important event for many island families between November and February. Starting in the early hours of the morning, families and friends gather for a long day of work to process every part of the pig into quality charcuterie and prime cuts that can be preserved for the year ahead. This community essence of sharing and making good use of every part of the animal is a continuing tradition for locals who are staunch conservationists of their protected islands' unique landscape and customs.

Working the land still provides a lifestyle that many islanders treasure and you will also see local olive oil production and expanses of fruit orchards, as well as sheep, goats, poultry and even snails. Some of the best-loved dishes from these island interiors make the most of this produce and you will often see meat paired with fruit or locally foraged ingredients. This might include succulent duck with roasted cherries (see page 207), a turkey roast perfectly matched with prunes (see page 240), chicken served with a rich chestnut sauce (see page 226) or garlic snails cooked with wild fennel (see page 229).

Perfect for winter or a long, lazy Sunday, this collection of recipes celebrates the slow-cooked braises, simmering rices, fideo pastas and local cuts that have nourished the carers of this special island landscape for generations.

COSTELLES DE CABRA ARREBOSSADES

Crumbed baby goat cutlets

SERVES 4

If you have access to goat, these finger-licking, crunchy, crumbed cutlets are a real specialty. Lamb works just as nicely, but try and get cutlets that haven't been Frenched. The eight ribs towards the top, closest to the loin, are quite tender, so they are reserved for whole racks. I've used individual cutlets, which are ideal for quick cooking in breadcrumbs. I serve them with hand-cut fries or a small fresh salad of whatever I have on hand, and then I add heaps of lemon and salt to the cutlets. I could eat these once a week, no problem!

120 g (4½ oz/2 cups) panko breadcrumbs
2 teaspoons finely chopped mint leaves
sea salt flakes and freshly ground black pepper
120 g (4½ oz) plain (all-purpose) flour
2 free-range eggs
1 tablespoon full-cream (whole) milk
1 kg (2 lb 3 oz) (about 12) small young goat or lamb cutlets
    (ask your butcher not to French-trim them)
200 ml (7 fl oz) light-flavoured extra virgin olive oil
2 rosemary sprigs
150 g (5½ oz) frisée lettuce (curly endive), leaves separated
2 tablespoons honey
lemon wedges, to serve

Blitz half the panko breadcrumbs in a food processor to a fine crumb. Transfer to a large shallow bowl and stir through the remaining breadcrumbs and mint. Season with salt and pepper.

Place the flour in a separate shallow bowl and in another, lightly beat the egg and milk.

Hold one of the cutlets at the top and dust in the flour, shaking off any excess, then dredge through the egg wash and roll in the breadcrumb mixture. Press the breadcrumbs into the cutlet to evenly coat, then transfer to a large tray. Repeat with the remaining cutlets.

Heat the oil and rosemary in a large frying pan over medium heat to 180°C (350°F) on a kitchen thermometer. Remove the rosemary from the oil when it starts to brown and sizzle, then, working in batches, add the cutlets and fry for 4–5 minutes on each side until golden and crisp. Transfer to a tray lined with paper towel to absorb the excess oil while you cook the remaining cutlets.

Place the cutlets on a large platter with the frisée. Sprinkle the cutlets with plenty of salt and a good drizzle of honey and serve with lemon wedges on the side.

ARRÒS DE MATANÇA

Seasonal hunter's rice

SERVE 4-6

A rural Ibizan winter ritual from times gone past, 'matança' – the day of the pig sacrifice – was undoubtedly the most festive day of the year. This social, reciprocal exchange and collaboration was held just before Christmas and brought together family, friends and neighbours for a long day of processing, which didn't end until the last sausages and salted meats were hung. Everyone had their role and expertise. The women would make 'bunyols' (doughnuts) for breakfast and serve up this hearty rice dish for lunch with the left-over cuts of pork, some chorizo and herbs.

2 tablespoons extra virgin olive oil
100 g (3½ oz) pork spare ribs, cut into 1.5 cm (½ in) dice
200 g (7 oz) pork fillet, cut into 2–3 cm (¾–1¼ in) chunks
1 pork and fennel sausage, sliced into 1 cm (½ in) rounds
1 fresh chorizo sausage, sliced into 1 cm (½ in) rounds
150 g (5½ oz) morcilla (Spanish black pudding), sliced into 1 cm (½ in) rounds
1 red capsicum (bell pepper), finely diced
1 green capsicum (bell pepper), finely diced
1 onion, finely chopped
3 garlic cloves, chopped
1 chicken liver, finely diced
1 teaspoon sweet pimentòn

1 teaspoon smoked pimentòn
1 cinnamon stick
125 ml (4 fl oz/½ cup) dry white wine
2 large tomatoes, grated, skins discarded
200 g (7 oz) short-grain rice, such as bomba or calasparra
1.5 litres (51 fl oz/6 cups) chicken stock, heated to a simmer
pinch of saffron
150 g (5½ oz) swiss brown or portobello mushrooms, cut into 2 cm (¾ in) chunks
150 g (5½ oz) pine or field mushrooms, cut into 2 cm (¾ in) chunks
200 g (7 oz) tinned butterbeans, rinsed and drained
lemon wedges, to serve

Heat half the oil in a 32–34 cm (12¾–13½ in) paella pan or frying pan over medium heat. Working in batches, cook the pork ribs and fillet, sausage, chorizo and morcilla for 5 minutes or until golden. Remove from the pan and set aside on a large plate.

Wipe out the paella pan with paper towel to remove any stuck-on bits and add the remaining oil, along with the red and green capsicum. Gently sauté over medium–low heat for 8–10 minutes, until soft and the colour has leached out of the capsicum into the oil. Using a slotted spoon, remove the capsicum from the pan and set aside on a small plate.

Add the onion, garlic and liver to the capsicum oil and cook for 12–15 minutes, until very soft and beginning to disintegrate. Stir in the pimentòns and cinnamon stick, then pour in the white wine and cook for 6–8 minutes, until completely evaporated. Add the grated tomato and cook for a further 15 minutes or until you have a rich, deep-coloured paste.

Add the rice and stir through to coat the grains. Return the reserved meat to the pan and stir through the cooked capsicum, three-quarters of the stock and the saffron. Bring to the boil, then reduce the heat to low and gently simmer for 10 minutes. If you're unable to achieve an even heat, rotate the pan around the burners on the stovetop so that each side of the pan cooks evenly. Pour in the remaining stock, add the mushrooms and butterbeans, then gently shake the pan from side to side. Check the bottom with a spoon if you fear it may be catching and reduce the heat, if possible. Continue to simmer over low heat for a further 8-10 minutes, until the rice is cooked through.

Remove from the heat and serve immediately in bowls with lemon wedges on the side.

FRITO MALLORQUIN

Mallorcan fry-up

SERVES 4–6

This Mallorcan dish is very popular among the locals. Like the 'trempó' salad on page 121, everything is cut up in equal-sized pieces, small enough so you can fit several ingredients in your mouth at once. The fennel really is a cleanser to the lamb's liver, so even if you think you're not a fan of offal, you might be pleasantly surprised! Or you could add more chilli, as this is one of the few spicy dishes on the island, although ease off if you're making it for a local. If you really do object to that strong meaty taste, just substitute the offal with more diced lamb and it will still be amazing.

Think of this as a Spanish stir-fry. It's best to use a wide-based saucepan, frying pan, wok or even a paella pan to give everything the space it needs to 'fry' instead of sweating too much. Also, 'jump' the pan as you go to keep the ingredients moving.

80 ml (2½ fl oz/⅓ cup) light-flavoured olive oil

80 ml (2½ fl oz/⅓ cup) extra virgin olive oil

4 medium potatoes, peeled and cut into 1 cm (½ in) dice

1 onion, diced

4 garlic cloves, unpeeled, smashed

sea salt flakes

2 teaspoons dry white wine

½ green capsicum (bell pepper), cut into 1 cm (½ in) dice

½ red capsicum (bell pepper), cut into 1 cm (½ in) dice

1 small fennel bulb, cut into 1 cm (½ in) dice, fronds reserved

1 small eggplant (aubergine), peeled in stripes lengthways, cut into 1 cm (½ in) dice

1 salad onion, diced

1 fresh bay leaf

2 marjoram or oregano sprigs

1–2 long red chillies, thickly sliced

200 g (7 oz) boneless lamb shoulder or leg, cut into 1 cm (½ in) dice

200 g (7 oz) lamb's or calf's liver, finely diced

freshly ground black pepper

Combine the oils in a jug and heat half the quantity in a large heavy-based saucepan over medium–high heat. Add the potato, onion, garlic and a pinch of salt and fry for 10–12 minutes, until the potato begins to soften and take on a golden colour.

Add the wine, capsicums, fennel, eggplant, salad onion, herbs and half the chilli, then increase the heat just a touch and cook for 12–15 minutes, stirring every few minutes to fry everything evenly without burning.

Meanwhile, in a separate frying pan, heat the remaining oil over high heat. Add the lamb and cook for 5 minutes, then add the liver with a pinch of salt and cook, stirring constantly, for 2 minutes, making sure not to overcook the liver. Strain off the oil in the pan and transfer the meat to the pan with the vegetables. Reduce the heat to medium and stir to bring everything together. Finish with the reserved fennel fronds and season with salt and pepper. Serve with the rest of the chilli scattered over the top, or more if you're keen.

POLLASTRE AMB MAGRANA

Pomegranate and fennel chicken

SERVES 4

This vibrant, tangy dish, which rings in autumn on the Balearic Islands, is another example of the Moorish influence on Spanish food. The use of fruits and nuts in Balearic cooking stems from Arabic occupation and many fruits and vegetables were introduced onto the islands at the time. If you look around closely, you'll even find remnants of dry-stone walls that form hillside terracing, along with surviving irrigation channels for agriculture, which are still used today.

This dish is a steadfast ode to the era and a sign of its long-lasting influence on Balearic daily life. It's also popularly made with quail or duck – another Moorish influence.

1 x 1.8 kg (4 lb) chicken, butterflied (ask your butcher to do this for you)
sea salt flakes and freshly ground black pepper
extra virgin olive oil
1 large onion, finely diced
4 garlic cloves, minced, plus 1 garlic bulb, halved crossways
1 fresh bay leaf
2 large pomegranates, arils removed
100 ml (3½ fl oz) pomegranate molasses

60 ml (2 fl oz/¼ cup) dry sherry
2 tablespoons brown sugar
1 red onion, sliced into 1.5 cm (½ in) thick rounds
2 thyme sprigs
1 fennel bulb, sliced into 1.5 cm (½ in) thick rounds, fronds reserved
2 teaspoons fennel seeds
25 g (1 oz) walnuts, roughly chopped
salad leaves, to serve

Season the chicken with salt and pepper and lay flat on a large plate. Transfer to the fridge for a minimum of 30 minutes, but preferably a few hours, to dry the skin a little.

Meanwhile, heat 1½ tablespoons of oil in a frying pan over medium heat and add the onion. Cook for 6–8 minutes, until starting to soften, then stir through the minced garlic and bay leaf. Cook for 2 minutes, then add half the pomegranate arils, the molasses, sherry and sugar. Bring to the boil, reduce the heat to low and gently simmer for 10–12 minutes, until the mixture has thickened and reduced by one-third. Remove and discard the bay leaf, then remove the pan from the heat and blitz the mixture with a hand-held blender until smooth. Pass the sauce through a fine sieve to remove the aril pulp and set aside in a bowl.

Preheat the oven to 220°C (430°F) fan-forced.

Place the red onion, garlic bulb, thyme and fennel in a large baking dish. Sprinkle with 2 tablespoons of the remaining pomegranate arils, drizzle over 1½ tablespoons of oil and season with salt and pepper. Place the butterflied chicken on top of the vegetables and rub with 1 tablespoon of oil. Sprinkle over the fennel seeds, season with salt and pepper, then transfer to the oven and roast for 15 minutes or until the skin starts to turn golden. Remove the dish from the oven and baste the top of the chicken with 2 tablespoons of the pomegranate sauce. Add 250 ml (8½ fl oz/1 cup) of water to the dish, then reduce the oven temperature to 160°C (320°F) and roast the chicken for a further 45 minutes.

Increase the temperature back to 220°C (430°F) and baste the chicken with 2 more tablespoons of sauce and add another 125 ml (4 fl oz/½ cup) of water to the dish. Bake for a final 6–8 minutes, until the chicken skin is dark and dry.

Meanwhile, in a small bowl, dress the chopped walnuts with a little olive oil and salt.

Transfer the roast chicken and caramelised fennel and onion to a serving platter and scatter over the the remaining pomegranate arils and the dressed walnuts. Serve with the remaining pomegranate sauce, the fennel fronds and a few salad leaves on the side.

MAGRET D'ÀNEC I CIRERES AL FORN

Duck breast with roasted cherries

SERVES 4

I first ate cherry jam as a young traveller in Mallorca during my first summer season working at The Sea Club in Cala Ratjada. I was on breakfast duty and responsible for skipping (sometimes crawling, depending on my previous night's explorations) up to the bakery to collect the bread order for the guests' morning buffet selection. Already 25°C (77°F) at 7 am, I'd rip open a croissant (made with lard, not butter) and use the jam as a dip to give me a good morning kick-start.

The chef at the time was a Jamie Oliver protégé and I would rush to polish the cutlery and get all my jobs done, so I could go in the kitchen and help prep the three-course dinner. It was my first job in a kitchen and I became hooked. This dish takes me back to that very special place and time. It goes really well with duck-fat potatoes or a creamy celeriac purée and some blanched green beans.

1 tablespoon extra virgin olive oil
4 duck breasts, fat scored
500 g (1 lb 2 oz) fresh or frozen cherries, pitted
40 g (1½ oz) butter, melted
1 tablespoon sherry vinegar
zest and juice of ½ orange
2 tablespoons brown sugar
1 teaspoon sea salt flakes
½ teaspoon white pepper

Preheat the oven to 200°C (400°F) fan-forced.

Heat half the oil in a large heavy-based frying pan and place the duck breasts, skin side down, in the pan. Cook for 4–6 minutes, until the skin is golden and blistering, then turn over and cook for a further 2–3 minutes, until golden and sealed. Transfer to a wire rack, fat side up, with a roasting tin underneath.

In a large bowl, toss the cherries with the butter, vinegar, orange zest and juice, sugar, salt and pepper. Transfer to a large baking dish and roast for 10 minutes.

At the same time, place the duck and the roasting tin in the oven and cook for 10–15 minutes, until cooked through to your liking, then remove and set aside to rest for 6–8 minutes.

Slice the duck breasts into four pieces and serve on a bed of the roasted cherries.

FIDEUÀ AMB PILOTES I PESOLS

Sobrassada meatballs with fideos and peas

SERVE 4–6

There are many types of fideo pasta used in various 'fideuà' dishes, particularly in Valencia, Catalunya and the Balearic provinces. 'Fideo' is the Spanish word for noodle and while the Western world might be more familiar with pasta via the Italians, these short noodles feature in some of Spain's most famous dishes, such as the squid ink fideo paella on page 166.

On the islands, this dish tends to be served quite wet, while the fideos are very well cooked. It's a comforting dish with the tasty sobrassada meatballs dotted among the soft pasta, and the mushrooms and cinnamon providing an earthy flavour. Cook it to your taste, but don't worry if you overcook the pasta, as that's how it's meant to be.

150 g (5½ oz) day-old crustless sourdough bread, torn into chunks
2 tablespoons full-cream (whole) milk
200 g (7 oz) minced (ground) pork
200 g (7 oz) minced (ground) veal
100 g (3½ oz) sobrassada
1 large free-range egg
1 teaspoon dried marjoram or oregano
sea salt flakes and freshly ground black pepper
3 tablespoons extra virgin olive oil
1 onion, chopped
3 garlic cloves, chopped
1 teaspoon sweet pimentòn
1 teaspoon smoked pimentòn
1 cinnamon stick
2 large tomatoes, grated, skins discarded

125 ml (4 fl oz/½ cup) dry white wine
150 g (5½ oz) swiss brown or portobello mushrooms, cut into 2 cm (¾ in) chunks
150 g (5½ oz) pine or field mushrooms, chopped into 2 cm (¾ in) chunks
1.2 litres (41 fl oz) chicken stock, heated to a simmer
pinch of saffron
200 g (7 oz) thick fideo pasta, or thick spaghetti cut into 2.5 cm (1 in) lengths
200 g (7 oz) tinned butterbeans, rinsed and drained
4 parsley sprigs, chopped
lemon wedges, to serve
crusty bread, to serve

Soak the bread in the milk in a small bowl for 5–10 minutes. Squeeze the milk from the bread and place the bread in a large bowl. Discard the milk.

Add the minced pork and veal, sobrassada, egg, marjoram or oregano and season with salt and pepper. With wet hands, roll the mixture into golf ball–sized balls.

Heat 1 tablespoon of the oil in a large frying pan over medium–high heat and fry the meatballs, swirling the pan to help keep them round, for 6–8 minutes, until evenly browned. Remove from the pan and set aside on a plate.

Add the remaining oil and the onion and cook for 8–10 minutes, until soft. Stir through the garlic, pimentòns and cinnamon stick and cook for a further 2 minutes, then add the grated tomato. Keep stirring, pour in the wine and simmer until evaporated. Add the mushrooms and continue to cook until beginning to colour. Add the chicken stock and saffron and bring to a rapid simmer. Add the fideo pasta and beans, then reduce the heat to a gentle simmer, cover and cook for 10–12 minutes. Return the meatballs to the pan and continue to cook for 6–8 minutes, until heated through and the pasta is very well cooked.

Ladle into serving bowls and stir through the chopped parsley. Serve with lemon wedges on the side and tuck in with some crusty bread.

PORC AMB FAVES OFEGADES

Braised pork and broad beans

SERVES 4

Broad (fava) beans make up a large part of the diet in Catalunya, Valencia and on the Balearic Islands. They're grown in garden beds to fix the nitrogen in the soil before tomatoes are planted, and harvested in spring as soon as they begin to sprout their pods. The sweet and earthy baby beans are used in salads or pickled, while any larger pods that have spent too long on the plant are best stewed in this meaty mountain dish, which is eaten after the 'matanças' (slaughtering season). A truly seasonal and holistic process, the acorns fall in autumn and fatten up the pigs throughout winter. Pork production then begins at the start of spring, coinciding nicely with the sprouting of the broad beans.

I cook this dish using broad beans at three stages in their life cycle. Unpodded broad beans give a great earthiness and thick texture to this stew, single-podded beans provide a bitter creaminess, while the naked green beans supply a nutty freshness.

1 kg (2 lb 3 oz) fresh broad (fava) beans
2 teaspoons butter
3 tablespoons extra virgin olive oil
4 x 200 g (7 oz) pork chops
100 g (3½ oz) pancetta, cut into 1.5 cm (½ in) dice
1 onion, thinly sliced
1 tablespoon sobrassada

3 garlic cloves, finely chopped
150 ml (5 fl oz) dry sherry or dry white wine
800 ml (27 fl oz) chicken stock
zest and juice of 1 lemon
2 mint sprigs, leaves picked
sea salt flakes and freshly ground black pepper
crusty bread, to serve

Divide the broad beans into three even piles. Double-pod one-third of the beans, single-pod another third and leave the remaining beans whole, trimming the ends if they're a bit scraggy.

Heat the butter and half the oil in a large heavy-based frying pan over high heat. Add the pork chops and cook for 4–6 minutes until golden and sealed on both sides. Transfer to a wire rack with a roasting tin underneath and set aside.

In the same pan, cook the pancetta and onion over medium–high heat for 6–8 minutes, until the onion is soft and translucent. Add the sobrassada and garlic and cook for 3–4 minutes, until the sobrassada has completely broken down.

Add the whole broad beans to the pan followed by the sherry or wine and bring to a simmer. Reduce the heat to medium and cook for 3–4 minutes, stirring the beans around to coat in the sauce.

Add the chicken stock and return the pork chops to the pan, along with the lemon zest. Cover with a tight-fitting lid and simmer for 12–15 minutes, until the beans are soft and wilted.

Stir through the single-podded beans and continue to simmer, covered, for another 8–10 minutes, until the skins begin to shrivel and shrink away from the beans. Increase the heat to high, add the final batch of beans and half the mint, and season with salt and pepper. Cook, uncovered, for 3–4 minutes, until the last batch of beans are soft but still green.

Divide the beans and pork chops among four serving plates, squeeze over the lemon juice and finish with the remaining mint. Serve with crusty bread on the side.

POLLASTRE FARCIT AMB SOBRASSADA

Roast chicken with sobrassada stuffing

SERVES 4

A Balearic Christmas Day is a traditional family feasting event, unlike in the rest of Spain where families come together on Christmas Eve. It's a time for stuffing: stockings, pastas, animals and pastries! The first course is usually 'sopa rellena', a stock-based broth with stuffed large pasta shells. Then you may see either suckling pig (see page 239) or roast turkey or chicken with a traditional stuffing, such as this recipe.

1 x 1.8 kg (4 lb) chicken
100 ml (3½ fl oz) grape juice (mosto) or verjuice
100 ml (3½ fl oz) sherry vinegar
100 ml (3½ fl oz) vi ranci or port
2 teaspoons chopped marjoram or oregano leaves
sea salt flakes and freshly ground black pepper
2 tablespoons extra virgin olive oil
1 large onion, finely diced
4 garlic cloves, minced
1 fresh bay leaf

2 tablespoons sobrassada or 1 fresh chorizo sausage, de-cased
200 g (7 oz) pork and fennel sausages, de-cased
30 g (1 oz/¼ cup) raisins
90 g (3 oz) black grapes, quartered
50 g (1¾ oz) freshly blitzed breadcrumbs
20 g (¾ oz) slivered almonds, toasted
½ teaspoon ground cinnamon
1 tablespoon chopped tarragon leaves
20 g (¾ oz) good-quality lard or butter
1 teaspoon honey

Rinse the chicken inside and out, then pat dry with paper towel. Transfer to a wire rack, breast side up, set over a roasting tin and place in the fridge for the skin to dry out a little.

Make a basting dressing in a bowl with the grape juice, vinegar, vi ranci or port and marjoram or oregano. Season with salt and pepper and set aside.

To make the stuffing, heat the oil in a frying pan over medium heat. Add the onion, garlic and bay leaf and cook for 12–15 minutes, until the onion is golden. Increase the heat to high and add the sobrassada, then stir through the sausage meat and cook, stirring, for 3–4 minutes. Transfer to a large bowl, add the raisins, grapes, breadcrumbs, almonds, cinnamon and tarragon and season with salt and pepper. Discard the bay leaf.

Preheat the oven to 180°C (350°F) fan-forced. Remove the chicken from the fridge.

Roll three-quarters of the stuffing into three large balls, compacting the mixture between your hands and squeezing to bind. Pack each ball tightly into the chicken. Wrap the remaining stuffing in baking paper and a layer of foil and set aside.

Rub the lard all over the chicken and pour half the basting dressing into the roasting tin with 250 ml (8½ fl oz/1 cup) of water. Roast for 45 minutes, then remove the tin and turn over the chicken. Give the liquid in the tin a stir and puncture a few holes into the chicken with a kitchen skewer. Baste the top of the chicken with 2 tablespoons of the dressing, then return to the oven, along with the remaining stuffing and roast for another 30 minutes.

Increase the temperature to 220°C (430°F) and remove the tin again. Turn the chicken back over and pierce a few more holes on each side of the spine. Baste with another 2 tablespoons of dressing and add a little more water to the tin if the liquid is drying out. Roast for another 8–10 minutes, until the skin is golden and crisp. Turn the oven off, open the door to let the heat out and leave the chicken to rest for 12–15 minutes.

Combine any remaining pan juices in a jug with the last of the dressing and the honey. Serve the chicken with the dressing and extra stuffing on the side.

SOBRASS

A symbol of identity for Balearic locals, sobrassada is a soft, spreadable, fermented pork sausage that's more like a pâté than chorizo, and much more versatile, too.

With Sicilian roots attributed to 'soppressata', this centuries-old cured meat was traditionally made by villagers as part of the late autumn 'matança', where every household slaughtered their own pigs and subsequently made an abundance of goods, including enough sobrassada to last the whole year.

Sobrassada was born out of a necessity to preserve meat in tricky climate conditions. The high humidity of the islands was not conducive to drier curing methods, so a fermentation process was adopted that kept the meat both moist and soft during the curing stage.

Today, as then, the sausages are made from a mix of lean pork meat, salted pork back fat (lardo), local pimentòns, black and white peppercorns and salt, all finely ground. The mixture is then stuffed into natural casings and hung in well-ventilated, open-air conditions out of direct sunlight to ferment at a moderate 16–18°C (61–64°F) from one to eight months, depending on their size.

Sobrassada is ideally made with the autochthonous black pig, 'porc negre', which has a higher fat content than its pink porcine cousins, which results in a softer, smoother cured sausage. Ibiza, Menorca and Mallorca all make their own sobrassada according to their own ways and traditions, and the sausages can have many different shapes, sizes and names, depending on when and where they are being consumed. Some are spicier than others, some add white pepper, while others will use black. The most common larger and fatter sausages, known as 'bisbe' (bishop), hail from Mallorca and have a longer curing time, meaning they aren't eaten until the summer months.

Eaten raw or cooked, on its own or added to a larger meal, sobrassada can be found in many local recipes. A true Balearic experience is to try it as a filling in that other emblematic island hero, the ensaïmada (see page 32). Other local dishes include sobrassada on toast with a drizzle of honey (see page 99) or fried and served with baked eggs. It's even used as a seasoning in traditional soups and stews. Try making croquettes with it, folding it through a root vegetable mash to add some funk or serve it in soft-shell tacos.

CONILL AMB CEBA

Rabbit and confit onion

SERVES 4

Everyone's Balearic grandma knows this one. On Mallorca, Menorca, Ibiza and Formentera there are plenty of rabbits and they have always made a hearty and sustainable meal in the leaner months. The onions sweeten and tenderise the tough meat in this farmhouse favourite, but it's also just as delicious with chicken, if you prefer.

1 rabbit, chopped into 8 pieces (ask your
   butcher to do this for you)
sea salt flakes and freshly ground black pepper
2 tablespoons extra virgin olive oil
4 garlic cloves, peeled
2 fresh bay leaves
1 kg (2 lb 3 oz) onions, sliced
2 whole cloves
10 black peppercorns

125 ml (4 fl oz/½ cup) Cognac
1 teaspoon dijon mustard
500 ml (17 fl oz/2 cups) chicken stock,
   heated to a simmer
micro herbs, to garnish (optional)

Hand-cut chips
4 all-purpose potatoes, cut into 2 cm (¾ in)
   thick chips
1 litre (34 fl oz/4 cups) vegetable oil,
   for deep-frying

Lightly season the rabbit with salt and pepper. Heat half the olive oil in a large heavy-based frying pan over high heat, add the rabbit and quickly sear for 1–2 minutes on all sides. Transfer to a plate and set aside.

Reduce the heat to medium–low, add the remaining oil and the garlic to the pan and cook on both sides until golden brown. Add the bay leaves and cook for 1 minute, then add the onion and a pinch of salt. Cover with a tight-fitting lid and cook for 12–15 minutes, until the onion is soft and translucent. Add the cloves, peppercorns and Cognac and stir through for a few minutes until the onion starts to take on a golden colour. Add the mustard and stock and return the rabbit to the pan. Cover with a lid and gently simmer for 40–50 minutes, until all the liquid has been absorbed and the onion and rabbit are the same colour.

Meanwhile, to make the chips, heat the oil in a large saucepan to 170°C (340°F) on a kitchen thermometer, Add the chips and fry, turning frequently, for 8–10 minutes, until just beginning to colour. Using a slotted spoon, transfer the chips to a plate lined with paper towel and place in the fridge for 20 minutes to cool down. Increase the oil temperature to 180°C (350°F) and fry the chips for a further 4–6 minutes, until light golden brown. Transfer to a plate lined with clean paper towel to soak up any excess oil, then sprinkle with salt.

Scatter a few micro herbs over the rabbit and onion, if you like, and serve with the chips on the side.

PERDIUS DE CAPELLÀ

Chaplain's (mock) partridges

SERVES 4

A curious title indeed! Originally from Menorca, this historic dish served throughout the Balearics doesn't contain partridges, or chaplains for that matter . . . It also goes by the name of 'feixets' and can be traced back more than 200 years. Back then, monasteries were poor and relied on meat offcuts to make their meals. This dish was made regal by rolling very thin slices of beef or veal around local charcuterie, probably the dried-out ends that needed cooking up. Full of flavour, these firm little parcels could easily pass for a small stuffed partridge under the dim lights of the church candelabra.

4 x 200 g (7 oz) veal escalopes
sea salt flakes and freshly ground black pepper
8 jamón slices
150 g (5½ oz) sobrassada or fresh chorizo
    sausage, de-cased
180 g (6½ oz) piece flat pancetta, cut into
    thin 1 cm (½ in) long batons
75 g (2¾ oz/½ cup) plain (all-purpose) flour
2 tablespoons extra virgin olive oil
4 garlic cloves, unpeeled, smashed

2 fresh bay leaves
1 onion, finely diced
1 small carrot, finely diced
1 tablespoon tomato paste (concentrated purée)
125 ml (4 fl oz/½ cup) Cognac
250 ml (8½ fl oz/1 cup) chicken stock, heated
    to a simmer
2 teaspoons chopped parsley or marjoram,
    to serve
mashed potato or crusty bread, to serve

Gently flatten one veal escalope with a meat cleaver to a 10 x 16 cm (4 x 6¼ in) rectangle. Cut it in half and set aside. Repeat with the remaining veal to make eight flattened escalopes.

Working with one escalope at a time, place on a clean work surface with a short end facing you. Lightly season and lay a slice of jamón over the top. Spoon 2 teaspoons of sobrassada or chorizo sausage in a log along the centre of the veal and scatter over a few pieces of pancetta. Fold over the side of the veal closest to you and roll up into an even log shape. Take some kitchen string and tie three or four lengths along the log to hold the filling in place when cooking. Repeat with the remaining escalopes to make eight parcels, then dust in the flour and set aside on a tray.

Heat half the oil in a large heavy-based frying pan over high heat. Add the stuffed veal and quickly sear on all sides. Transfer to a plate and set aside.

Reduce the heat to medium–low and add the remaining oil, along with the garlic, bay leaves, onion, carrot and a pinch of salt. Cook for 15 minutes or until the vegetables are soft and beginning to break down, then add the tomato paste and cook for 4–5 minutes, until it turns dark red and the pan starts to dry out. Pour in the Cognac, allow to simmer and reduce slightly, then add the stock. Cook for 3–4 minutes to bring the flavours together, then remove the bay leaves and blitz the mixture with a hand–held blender to a smooth sauce.

Return the stuffed veal to the pan, cover with a tight-fitting lid and cook for 8–10 minutes, turning the veal over halfway.

Remove the kitchen string from the veal and scatter over the parsley or marjoram. Serve with your favourite mash and some crusty bread.

SOFRIT PAGÈS

Farmer's pot

SERVES 4

A festive specialty of the Pitiuses, which includes the islands of Ibiza and Formentera, this farmer's pot was once considered too expensive to eat regularly. Unlike fish, which locals caught for themselves and maybe a neighbour, or an inexpensive island chicken, the ingredients in the dish made it a special once-a-year, if that, occasion. A mix of meats, seasonal vegetables and local herbs and spices from the garden would be traditionally cooked at Christmas time on inland local farms, but today you'll find it on menus at local restaurants showing off their wares.

1 kg (2 lb 3 oz) bone-in lamb neck or shoulder, cut into 8 pieces (ask your butcher to do this for you)
4 fresh bay leaves
2 skinless chicken thigh cutlets, cut in half
250 ml (8½ fl oz/1 cup) extra virgin olive oil
2 good-quality pork sausages, cut into 8 pieces
2 fresh chorizo sausages, cut into 8 pieces
½ green capsicum (bell pepper), diced
½ red capsicum (bell pepper), diced
1 onion, sliced
3 tomatoes, roughly chopped
2 marjoram or oregano sprigs

1 teaspoon sweet pimentòn
2 small garlic bulbs
500 g (1 lb 2 oz) chat (baby) potatoes
2 small marinated artichoke hearts, halved
freshly ground black pepper

Picada
3 small garlic cloves, finely chopped
pinch of sea salt flakes
1 bunch curly parsley, leaves picked and chopped
2 teaspoons dry white wine
80 ml (2½ fl oz/⅓ cup) light-flavoured olive oil
30 ml (1 fl oz) grapeseed oil

To make the picada, combine the ingredients in a bowl and set aside.

Blanch the lamb in a large saucepan of simmering salted water with one bay leaf for 40 minutes. In a separate saucepan of simmering salted water, add the chicken and another bay leaf and cook for 25 minutes. Strain the liquids into one large stockpot and set aside the lamb and chicken on a large plate. Simmer the meat broth for 30–40 minutes, until reduced by half.

Heat 1 tablespoon of the oil in a large heavy-based frying pan over high heat. Working in batches, sear the lamb and chicken on all sides, then transfer to a heavy-based stockpot. Cook the sausage and chorizo in the same pan until golden brown on all sides, then transfer to the pot with the cooked meat.

Add the capsicums and onion to the pan and cook over medium–low heat for 12–15 minutes, until soft and starting to colour. Add the tomato, another bay leaf, the marjoram or oregano and pimentòn, and cook, stirring to combine, for 6–8 minutes, until the tomato has broken down to a paste. Stir through half the picada and add 1.25 litres (42 fl oz/5 cups) of the reserved broth. Bring to a simmer, then transfer to the pot with the meat.

Meanwhile, in a separate frying pan, heat the remaining oil over medium–low heat and add the garlic, potatoes and the remaining bay leaf. Sauté for 20–30 minutes, until the potatoes are cooked through and golden. Transfer the potatoes and garlic to a tray lined with paper towel to absorb any residual oil, then transfer to the pot with the meats and stock.

Still over medium–low heat, fry the artichoke for 2 minutes or until golden brown, then add to the pot. Stir through 2 tablespoons of the remaining picada and place the pot over medium–high heat. Bring to a simmer, season with salt and pepper, then cover and cook for 10 minutes to bring all the flavours together.

Serve on a large platter with the remaining picada spooned over the top.

ARRÒS BRUT

Dirty rice

SERVES 4–6

There's nothing unclean about this dish! The title refers to the rustic, seasonal and intensely flavoured nature of this Mallorcan winter tradition. The island cousin of the paella, dirty rice shares its family roots with a good 'sofrito', as all good Spanish rice dishes do. It's made with whatever is seasonally on hand, so you might find thrushes, quail or partridge (giblets and all) included, along with snails, vegetable-patch pickings or wild mushrooms which, along with a distinct blend of spices, contribute to that 'dirty', earthy flavour.

2 tablespoons extra virgin olive oil
1 pork spare rib, cut into 1.5 cm
    (½ in) dice
200 g (7 oz) chicken ribs
200 g (7 oz) rabbit (or use a boneless chicken
    thigh fillet), cut into 2–3 cm (¾–1¼ in) chunks
4 artichoke hearts in brine, halved
1 red capsicum (bell pepper), thinly sliced
1 onion, chopped
3 garlic cloves, chopped
1 tablespoon sobrassada or 2 teaspoons
    sweet pimentòn
125 ml (4 fl oz/½ cup) dry white wine
2 large tomatoes, grated, skins discarded
400 g (14 oz) short-grain rice, such
    as bomba or calasparra

1.5 litres (51 fl oz/6 cups) chicken stock,
    heated to a simmer
pinch of saffron
8–12 prepared snails (optional)
8 asparagus spears, cut into 2 cm (¾ in) lengths
150 g (5½ oz) runner (flat) beans, trimmed, cut
    into 2 cm (¾ in) lengths
100 g (3½ oz/⅔ cup) frozen peas
lemon wedges, to serve

Spice mix
¼ teaspoon ground cinnamon
¼ teaspoon ground cloves
¼ teaspoon freshly ground nutmeg
¼ teaspoon ground allspice
¼ teaspoon freshly ground black pepper

Combine the spice mix ingredients in a small bowl and set aside.

Heat half the oil in a large 32–34 cm (12¾–13½ in) paella pan or frying pan over medium heat. Working in batches, cook the pork, chicken, rabbit and artichoke until seared and golden brown on all sides. Remove from the pan and set aside on a large plate.

Wipe out the paella pan to remove any stuck-on bits, then add the remaining oil along with the capsicum and gently sauté over medium–low heat for 8–10 minutes, until soft and the colour has leached out of the capsicum into the oil. Remove the capsicum from the pan and set aside on a small plate.

Add the onion and garlic to the pan and cook over medium–low heat for 12–15 minutes, until soft and beginning to disintegrate. Stir through the sobrassada or pimentòn along with the spice mix and cook for 3–4 minutes, then pour in the white wine and cook for 6–8 minutes, until completely evaporated. Add the grated tomato and cook for a further 15 minutes or until the mixture becomes a rich, deep-coloured thick paste. Add the rice and stir to coat the grains. Stir through the reserved meats, artichoke and capsicum, along with three-quarters of the stock and the saffron.

Bring the mixture to the boil, then reduce the heat to low and simmer for 10 minutes. If you're unable to achieve an even heat, rotate the pan around the burners on the stovetop so that each side of the pan cooks evenly. Pour in the remaining stock, add the snails (if using), asparagus and beans and gently shake the pan from side to side. Check the bottom with a spoon if you fear it may be catching and reduce the heat, if possible. Continue to simmer for 8–10 minutes, until the rice is cooked through. Scatter over the peas and cook for a final 2 minutes.

Remove from the heat and serve immediately with lemon wedges on the side.

POLLASTRE AMB SALSA DE CASTANYES

Chestnut chicken

SERVES 4

Traditionally this dish is made with game, as the island autumn chestnuts lend themselves well to the stronger flavours of partridge, pheasant or even pigeon. I like any excuse to cook and serve game, especially as chicken can get a little boring throughout the year, but this sauce is special enough to grab a good ol' free-range chook and turn it into this island specialty.

800 g (1 lb 12 oz) fresh chestnuts
60 g (2 oz) butter
2 tablespoons extra virgin olive oil
1 x 1.6 kg (3½ lb) chicken, chopped into 10 pieces
    (ask your butcher to do this for you)
1 medium leek, white part only, thinly sliced
sea salt flakes
2 garlic cloves, thinly sliced (or use young garlic shoots
    if you can get them)
2 thyme sprigs, plus thyme leaves to serve
60 ml (2 fl oz/¼ cup) dry sherry
2 litres (2 qts) chicken stock, heated to a simmer
150 ml (5 fl oz) pouring (single/light) cream
¼ teaspoon freshly grated nutmeg
freshly ground black pepper

Preheat the oven to 180°C (350°F) fan-forced.

Using a small serrated knife, score the top of each chestnut with a cross. Wrap the chestnuts in foil and transfer to a wire rack set over a roasting tin and roast for 20–25 minutes, until they begin to split open.

Transfer the chestnuts to a large heatproof bowl and cover with plastic wrap for 10 minutes to steam and sweat. Peel the chestnuts and set two or three aside for garnish. Discard the shells.

Heat the butter and half the oil in a large heavy-based saucepan over medium–high heat. Add the chicken and sear each side for 4–6 minutes, until golden. Transfer to a plate and set aside.

In the same pan, add the leek and a pinch of salt and cook, stirring occasionally, for 4–6 minutes, until softened. Stir through the garlic and thyme and cook for 2 minutes, then add the sherry and simmer until evaporated. Add the peeled chestnuts and stir to coat in the sauce, then pour in the chicken stock. Increase the heat to high and simmer for 20 minutes or until the liquid has reduced by one-third. Reduce the heat to low, remove the thyme sprigs, then carefully blend the mixture using a hand-held blender. Return the chicken to the pan and simmer for a further 20–25 minutes or longer for a thicker sauce.

Stir through the cream and nutmeg and season with salt and pepper. Serve with the thyme leaves and reserved chestnuts crumbled on top.

CARGOLS AMB ALL I FONOLL

Garlic snails with fennel

SERVES 4

Eaten in Mallorca at the yearly celebration of Sant Marc, Balearic snails are a lot skinnier and smaller than those found on the mainland or in France. They're cooked with a 'sofrito' base, different cuts of chicken and pork and locally picked herbs for several hours in a huge stockpot to really tenderise the meat.

I've gone for a less traditional, but still local-flavoured, recipe to showcase the earthiness of the snails while keeping things simple. You will always find a little spice served with snails over there – whether it be from an overdose of garlic, black pepper or chilli itself – to help dissipate the muddy flavour of the snails, along with a good dollop of allioli for dipping.

1½ tablespoons extra virgin olive oil
120 g (4½ oz) pancetta, very finely diced
½ onion, super finely diced
½ fennel bulb, super finely diced, fronds reserved and chopped
1 garlic bulb, plus 3 garlic cloves, finely chopped
2 thyme sprigs
60 ml (2 fl oz/¼ cup) dry sherry

400 ml (13½ fl oz) chicken stock or water
200 g (7 oz) tinned snails in brine, rinsed and drained
1 teaspoon anise liqueur
1 teaspoon sea salt flakes
½ teaspoon freshly ground black pepper
½ teaspoon white pepper
36 large snail shells (optional)
crusty baguette, to serve

Heat the oil and pancetta in a frying pan over medium–high heat and cook for 4–5 minutes, until the pancetta starts to crackle and pop. Add the onion, fennel, garlic bulb and thyme, reduce the heat to medium–low and cook, stirring every now and then, for 20 minutes or until the onion and fennel are soft and beginning to disintegrate. Stir through the chopped garlic and cook, stirring constantly, for 2 minutes. Pour in the sherry and cook until the liquid evaporates, then add the stock and snails and simmer, covered, for 20–25 minutes, until the garlic bulb has softened.

Remove the garlic bulb and transfer to a wire rack for 5–10 minutes, until cool enough to handle. Peel the garlic, place in a mortar and pestle or small bowl and pound or mash to a smooth purée.

Stir the garlic paste back through the snails and continue to simmer until the liquid has reduced by half and started to thicken. Stir through the anise liqueur and season with the salt and both peppers. Add the reserved fennel fronds, then remove from the heat and, using a spoon, stuff each snail shell (if using) with one snail and a spoonful of sauce. Arrange in a shallow bowl or serve the snails and their sauce as they are in a bowl with some ripped baguette and a small glass of anise liqueur.

LLENTIES I FORMATGE DE CABRA AMB GUATLLES ESCABETXADES

Lentil and goat's cheese salad with pickled quail

SERVES 4–6

In the old days, Balearic Island cheese was usually thrown together with whatever milk was available – usually a combination of sheep's and goat's milk with no real regard to ratios. Milk thistle was, and still is, used instead of rennet, giving the cheese its distinct bitter–sour flavours. From the same family as the artichoke, milk thistle flowers in the summer and is harvested on the island once it dries. It's then stored and rehydrated in time for cheese-making. The liquid used to rehydrate the thistle becomes the curdling agent that separates the milk solids from the whey. These curds are then salted, pressed and matured for different amounts of time. The freshest, or youngest, cheese is usually reserved for baking, but I love to use it in this salad, as it almost acts like a thick dressing, coating the lentils.

This salad can also be served warm on cooler days.

4 x Pickled quail (see page 80)
300 g (10½ oz) dried green or brown lentils
1 fresh bay leaf
2 thyme sprigs
3 tablespoons extra virgin olive oil
½ bunch rainbow silverbeet (Swiss chard), stalks finely chopped, leaves thinly sliced
2 garlic cloves, chopped

sea salt flakes and freshly ground black pepper
1½ teaspoons dijon mustard
juice of ½ lemon
2 teaspoons sherry or red wine vinegar
½ red onion, finely diced
2 tablespoons chopped mint leaves, plus extra leaves to serve
120 g (4½ oz) goat's curd or goat's feta

Remove the quail from their pickling liquid and bring to room temperature.

Rinse the lentils and place in a large stockpot with the bay leaf and thyme. Cover with three times as much cold water as the lentils, then bring to a simmer over medium heat. Cook for 20–30 minutes, until the lentils are just tender, but not falling apart. Remove from the heat and transfer the lentils and their cooking liquid to a baking dish to cool down a little. If they are really tender, skip this process and drain them straight away. Rinse the lentils under cold water if they are already starting to fall apart. You will compromise the flavour, but you won't be left with mushy lentils.

Meanwhile, heat half the oil in a frying pan over medium heat, add the silverbeet stalks and garlic and sauté for 3–4 minutes. Transfer to a plate and set aside. Add the silverbeet leaves and sauté for 1–2 minutes, until just wilted. Set aside on the same plate with the stalks and season with salt and pepper.

In a small bowl, make a dressing with the mustard, lemon juice, vinegar, the remaining oil and salt and pepper, to taste.

Once the lentils have cooled slightly, drain and transfer to a large bowl. Toss through the dressing while the lentils are still warm. Set aside to cool down further, then mix through the silverbeet, onion and mint.

Divide the lentils among bowls, then top with a pickled quail, the goat's curd and a few mint leaves. Drizzle over some of the pickling liquid and a few extra vegetables from the pickled quail, if you like, and serve.

XAI A LA CERVESA

Beer-braised lamb shanks

SERVES 4

Traditionally this dish was cooked in local beer made with farmers' hops and honey from the land, making it a much-loved island classic. Today, thanks to the tourists' palate, a lot of good German beers can be found in Mallorca and increasingly there are also a number of cool, local craft-beer companies making their way into bars, restaurants and hotels.

This dish normally uses a whole lamb shoulder chopped up by the local butcher, but I've used shanks here for ease and uniformity.

4 x 375 g (13 oz) lamb shanks
sea salt flakes and freshly ground black pepper
2 tablespoons light-flavoured extra virgin olive oil
150 g (5½ oz) pancetta, diced
2 celery stalks, finely diced
1 carrot, finely diced
3 garlic cloves, finely chopped
2 rosemary sprigs, leaves picked
8 spring onions (scallions), white part only, roughly chopped
330 ml (11 fl oz) bottle strong lager or beer
1 litre (34 fl oz/4 cups) chicken or vegetable stock

Score three or four slits in the flesh of each shank and season with salt and pepper.

Preheat the oven to 180°C (350°F) fan-forced.

Heat half the oil in a flameproof casserole dish over high heat, add the lamb shanks and sear on all sides, until golden. Transfer the lamb to a plate and set aside.

Wipe out the pan to remove any remaining stuck-on bits and reduce the heat to medium–high. Add the remaining oil and the pancetta and cook for 4–5 minutes, until beginning to crisp, then add the celery and carrot and cook for 12–15 minutes, until soft. Add the garlic, rosemary and spring onion, stir for 2 minutes, then add the beer and simmer until the liquid reduces to a syrup.

Pour in the stock, bring to the boil, then reduce the heat to medium and simmer for 5 minutes. Return the lamb to the pan, cover and place in the oven for 30 minutes. Reduce the temperature to 160°C (320°F) and bake for a further 1½ hours. Increase the temperature back up to 180°C (350°F), remove the lid and cook for a final 30 minutes or until the tops of the shanks colour slightly and the sauce has reduced a little.

Serve the lamb shanks with your favourite purée, such as celeriac, parsnip, cauliflower or good old-fashioned mashed potato and loads of sauce, and wash it all down with a nice cold beer.

RAGOUT DE XAI

Chunky lamb ragout

SERVES 4

The French briefly wrestled Menorca from the British in the 18th century before it was finally returned to Spain during The French Revolutionary Wars. This slow-cooked lamb stew is a result of that brief French influence on the island. Like the French 'navarin printanier' (spring stew), except without the turnips and with the addition of pimentòn, this dish requires little effort. You can make it the day before and have it ready to go the next day, or put it all in the slow cooker and forget about it.

3 tablespoons extra virgin olive oil
3 garlic cloves, unpeeled, smashed
1 kg (2 lb 3 oz) boneless lamb shoulder, cut into 8 pieces
1 rack of lamb, cut into 4 double-rib cutlets
1½ onions, finely diced
1 large carrot, finely diced
8 French shallots, peeled
1 fresh bay leaf
2 thyme sprigs
3 marjoram or oregano sprigs
1 rosemary sprig
1 teaspoon sweet pimentòn
1 teaspoon ground coriander
1 teaspoon ground fennel
½ teaspoon white pepper
1 teaspoon sea salt flakes

1 tablespoon plain (all-purpose) flour
3 tomatoes, grated, skins discarded
1 tablespoon tomato paste (concentrated purée)
60 ml (2 fl oz/¼ cup) brandy or Cognac
1 litre (34 fl oz/4 cups) beef stock
1 bunch Dutch carrots, peeled
155 g (5½ oz/1 cup) frozen peas

Mashed potato
1 kg (2 lb 3 oz) sebago, yukon gold or Dutch cream potatoes, peeled and cut into 4 cm (1½ in) chunks
1 teaspoon fine sea salt
1 fresh bay leaf
125 ml (4 fl oz/½ cup) full-cream (whole) milk
30 g (1 oz) salted butter
60 ml (2 fl oz/¼ cup) extra virgin olive oil
freshly ground black pepper

Heat half the oil and the garlic in a large heavy-based saucepan over medium–high heat. Add the lamb pieces and cutlets and sear on all sides until golden. Transfer to a plate and set aside.

Reduce the heat to medium–low and add the remaining oil, the onion, carrot, shallot, herbs, spices, salt and flour. Sauté for 10 minutes or until soft and starting to colour.

Stir through the tomato and tomato paste and cook for 2 minutes, then add the brandy, followed by the stock. Gently simmer, semi-covered, for 1 hour. Add the Dutch carrots and cook for a further 8–10 minutes, then stir through the peas in the final 5 minutes of cooking.

Meanwhile, to make the mashed potato, place the potato in a large saucepan and cover with cold water. Add the salt and bay leaf, then bring to the boil, reduce the heat and simmer for 15–20 minutes, until the potato is soft and cooked through. Drain and set aside in a large bowl, discarding the bay leaf.

Warm the milk and butter in a microwave or small saucepan over medium heat until the butter is melted and the milk is warmed through. Pour over the potato and mash until smooth. Add 1 tablespoon of the oil and, using a wooden spoon, beat into the mash until fully incorporated. Add the remaining oil in two batches, then season with salt and pepper.

Divide the mashed potato among plates and top with the lamb ragout.

PORCELLA

Suckling pig

SERVES 6–8

'Lechona', as it is also fondly known in Spanish, is suckling pig spit-roasted over a wood-fired rotisserie. Working at The Sea Club in Cala Ratjada, Mallorca, a few summer seasons in a row, one of my favourite things to do on my only night off was to go up to the old castle tower in Canyamel to the restaurant Porxada de Sa Torre and sit with the rest of the crew and some of the guests at a big old medieval table and devour a suckling pig or two! Said to be the best 'porcella' on the island, the individual plates themselves were almost the size of a baby's bath. Traditionally served whole, the suckling pig is chopped up in front of you using the edge of a plate! That's my kind of night out.

Hire or borrow a spit-roaster for this feast – you may get two to three whole piglets on there depending on their size. Or you can still do this recipe in an oven – just cook the pig at 220°C (430°F) fan-forced on the bottom shelf over a large roasting tin, and baste with olive oil and pan juices every 20 minutes for 2½ hours.

extra virgin olive oil
1 x 5–6 kg (11 lb–13 lb 4 oz) suckling pig
fine sea salt and freshly ground black pepper
500 g (1 lb 2 oz) fresh or frozen cherries, pitted
60 g (2 oz) butter, melted
1 tablespoon sherry vinegar

1 loaf sourdough, ripped into large chunks
3 apples, cored and chopped
1 tablespoon chopped rosemary plus 1 bunch
   rosemary, tied with kitchen string
8 garlic cloves, finely chopped
1 teaspoon white pepper

Fire up your coals 1–1½ hours before you start cooking. You want the coals to be white with no flame.

Massage a few tablespoons of the oil into the pig skin and season liberally, both inside and out, with plenty of salt and black pepper.

Combine the cherries, butter, vinegar, bread, apple, chopped rosemary, garlic and white pepper in a large bowl. Spread this mixture in the cavity of the pig (any left-overs can be wrapped in foil and thrown in the coals for 30 minutes), then sew up the pig with thick kitchen string or thin wire to hold the stuffing in.

Mount the pig on the spit – they all vary slightly, so just make sure it is well secured on the axle and doesn't slide around – and start rotating.

Distribute the hot coals, so the majority are at the edges of the pit and under the thickest part of the pig (beneath the shoulders and rump). Using the bunch of rosemary as a brush, apply a good basting of oil every 20 minutes.

As the stuffing starts to cook, moisture may start to leak from the closed cavity, but the bread should catch most of it. Wipe any wetter spots with paper towel to keep the skin dry for even crackling.

After 1½–1¾ hours of rotation, lower the pig closer to the coals for 30 minutes to crisp up and darken the crackling. Turn the rotation off and test the shoulder or leg meat with a thermometer – it should be 70–75°C (160–165°F). Cook for a little longer, if necessary.

Dismount the spit using thick oven gloves and hold a large platter beneath the pig as it can quickly slide off the spit.

Serve whole if you have a large enough board or platter or chop up and serve as part of a larger feast.

ROSTIT D'INDIOT

Turkey roast with prunes and pine nuts

SERVES 6

This is not your typical Anglo-Saxon Christmas or Thanksgiving turkey roast. In this dish, the turkey is butchered into smaller cuts, braised in a rich 'sofrito' and then finished with prunes and a traditional 'picada' of almonds. It's a Christmas Day favourite around the Balearic Islands with a subtly sweet and well-balanced flavour. Turkey was historically only eaten by the noble elite as poultry was too expensive for the islands' poor, and even now this dish will only be brought out for special family feasts or Christmas.

120 g (4½ oz) blanched almonds, blitzed
   to a fine crumb
2 teaspoons chopped marjoram or oregano
½ turkey (about 1.8 kg/4 lb), cut into 12 pieces
   (ask your butcher to do this for you)
150 g (5½ oz/1 cup) plain (all-purpose) flour
2 teaspoons sweet pimentòn
sea salt flakes and freshly ground black pepper
60 ml (2 fl oz/¼ cup) extra virgin olive oil
2 onions, diced

4 garlic cloves, peeled and smashed
1 fresh bay leaf
2 tomatoes, finely diced
3 tablespoons brandy
1.5 litres (51 fl oz/6 cups) chicken stock,
   plus extra if needed
8–12 small chat (baby) potatoes, peeled
12 pitted prunes
25 g (1 oz) pine nuts
crusty bread, to serve

Preheat the oven to 180°C (350°F) fan-forced.

Using a mortar and pestle or a blender, pound or blitz the almonds and marjoram or oregano to a fine paste. Set aside.

Dust the turkey with the flour and pimentòn and season with salt and pepper.

Heat the oil in an extra-large flameproof casserole dish over medium–high heat. Add the turkey and sear the pieces on all sides until golden. Transfer to a plate.

Reduce the heat to medium, add the onion, garlic and bay leaf to the dish with a pinch of salt and sauté for 10–12 minutes, until soft and starting to colour. Stir through the tomato and cook for 6 minutes or until beginning to caramelise, then pour in the brandy. Cook until the liquid has evaporated, then return the turkey to the dish, along with the stock. Transfer to the oven and roast for 1¼–1½ hours.

Remove the dish from the oven and add the potatoes. Stir through the almond paste, prunes and pine nuts. Add a little more stock or water if the dish is looking dry.

Cover the dish and cook for a further 20–25 minutes, until the potato is cooked through and the liquid has reduced to a thick sauce.

Serve with a big basket of crusty bread and a few glasses of Cava.

LLOM AMB COL

Brined pork and cabbage

SERVES 4

This dish is a combination of European cuisines, with the distinctly strong pork flavour pairing beautifully with the sweet cabbage and earthy mushrooms. The brining is not absolutely essential, but I love how it imparts even more flavour to the dish and prevents the loin from drying out, culminating in a moist, evenly cooked result every time.

1 kg (2 lb 3 oz) pork loin, skin on and scored
2 tablespoons light-flavoured extra virgin
    olive oil
sea salt flakes
¼ green or savoy cabbage, outer leaves removed
120 g (4½ oz) pancetta, diced
½ onion, finely diced
2 celery stalks, finely diced
¼ fennel bulb, finely diced, fronds reserved
3 garlic cloves, chopped
150 g (5½ oz) swiss brown or pine mushrooms,
    finely chopped
3 thyme sprigs
150 ml (5 fl oz) dry sherry or dry white wine

750 ml (25½ fl oz/3 cups) chicken or
    vegetable stock
freshly ground black pepper
crusty bread, to serve

Brine
1 tablespoon black or white peppercorns
1 tablespoon aniseed
1 tablespoon fennel seeds
70 g (2½ oz) fine sea salt
55 g (2 oz/¼ cup) brown sugar
2 fresh bay leaves
250 ml (8½ fl oz/1 cup) boiling water
270 g (9½ oz) ice cubes

To make the brine, lightly toast the spices in a small frying pan over medium heat, until fragrant and just starting to smoke. Place in a large non-reactive dish with the salt, sugar and bay leaves and pour in the boiling water. Stir until the salt and sugar have dissolved, then add the ice and stir until it has mostly melted. Add the pork to the brine, skin side up, and top up with extra cold water to cover the loin (but not the skin), if necessary. Refrigerate for 12 hours, then drain the pork and thoroughly pat dry with paper towel to remove as much moisture as possible. Set aside, uncovered, to continue drying out.

Preheat the oven to 230°C (445°F) fan-forced.

Once the pork has come to room temperature, place it on a wire rack, skin side up, over a roasting tin and rub in half the oil and a good sprinkling of salt. Roast for 30–40 minutes, until starting to crackle on top. Reduce the heat to 170°C (340°F) and continue to cook for 40–45 minutes, until the juice of the loin runs clear when pierced with a skewer.

Meanwhile, cut the cabbage into four wedges with the core attached to hold them together.

Heat the remaining oil in a large frying pan over high heat. Add the cabbage and cook on each side for 4–6 minutes, until golden, then remove from the pan and transfer to a large baking dish.

Reduce the heat to medium–high and fry off the pancetta for 4–5 minutes, until beginning to crisp, then add the onion, celery and fennel and cook for 12–15 minutes, until soft. Add the garlic, mushroom and thyme and cook, stirring frequently, for 8–10 minutes, until golden. Pour in the sherry or wine and simmer until the liquid has reduced to a syrup. Add the stock, bring to the boil, then reduce the heat to medium and simmer for 15–20 minutes, until the liquid has reduced by half. Spoon into the baking dish with the cabbage.

Increase the oven temperature to 230°C (445°F). Roast the cabbage on the bottom shelf of the oven for 10 minutes or until soft.

Rest the pork for 12–15 minutes, then slice and divide among plates. Place the roasted cabbage on a serving platter, top with the fennel fronds and serve.

TRES

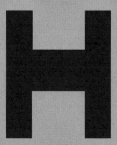**H**istorically, Balearic desserts were simple dishes eaten to aid digestion and prevent any side effects from over-eating. Usually reserved for the rich or given to the gods in the form of dried fruit, honey, cheese or nuts, the evolution of the final course has come a long way, and today these desserts are as special as any seen on the mainland.

There are, however, still hints of tradition and many island desserts feature local ingredients, such as aniseed, almonds, cinnamon, fruit and fresh curds and cheeses. Locally sourced honey still remains a popular sweetener on the islands, as sugar was deemed too expensive in the past.

Desserts don't feature heavily in the Balearic daily diet; instead they are reserved for Christian festivals, special occasions or as an homage to one of the many periods of foreign occupation on the islands. French and British influences can be found throughout the Balearic dessert repertoire, but they will always be served with a Spanish twist. This might include a lemon meringue tart made with a cookie base instead of pastry (see page 264), a bread pudding using day-old ensaïmadas (see page 249) or a custard flan, scented with orange and cinnamon (see page 253). The Spanish love for nougat (turrón) is also ever-present. Arabic in origin, these simple baked goods were a way to use up the yearly surplus of almonds and fruit. 'Turróns' may be soft, chewy or hard and they are still presented at Christmas and other festivals as gifts for loved ones.

In the past, the only ovens available on the islands were the wood-fired kilns in the towns' bakeries. Inhabitants would come together once a week to collectively bake and share food. Many of the islands' star desserts are still baked in traditional 'greixeras' – heatproof, porous earthenware dishes that can withstand high heat, while ensuring gentle, even cooking from the outside in. From the prized baked ricotta cheesecake made in all Mallorcan homes (see page 254) and Ibiza's famous mint and aniseed 'flaò' (flan) (see page 258) to a pumpkin pie served with fresh lemon (see page 263), you may well discover it's worth investing in a good-quality, ceramic vessel to achieve that classic island taste. It will surely become a well-loved addition to your kitchen and it makes a great presentation dish, too.

The recipes in this chapter make the perfect end to an evening meal, served either on their own or as a digestif with coffee. Simple to make, these timeless classics will transport you back to that sunset meal looking out over the ocean or that late-night treat with your favourite tipple.

GREIXONERA

Balearic pudding

SERVES 6

'Greixonera' is a much-loved and cherished dessert eaten across the Balearic Islands. Its name refers to the earthenware vessel in which it is baked, while the dish itself was born out of a culture of zero waste as a way to use up the previous day's ensaïmadas. Failing access to this Balearic pastry, you can do as the French and British do and use croissants, sponge cake, sweet buns or any bread-based pastries you can get your hands on. Even hot cross buns make a great greixonera!

1 litre (34 fl oz/4 cups) full-cream (whole) milk
300 g (10½ oz) caster (superfine) sugar, plus extra for sprinkling
1 cinnamon stick
peel of ½ lemon, white pith removed
peel of ½ orange, white pith removed
7 large free-range eggs
½ teaspoon ground cinnamon
5 small Ensaïmadas (see page 32) or croissants
20 g (¾ oz) unsalted butter, softened

Preheat the oven to 170°C (340°F) fan-forced.

Gently warm the milk, sugar, cinnamon stick and citrus peels in a saucepan over medium–low heat until just simmering. Remove from the heat and set aside for 15 minutes for the flavours to infuse. Once cooled slightly, remove and discard the cinnamon stick and citrus peels.

Whisk the eggs and ground cinnamon in a large heatproof bowl.

Slowly pour the milk mixture into the beaten eggs, whisking to combine.

Tear the sweet pastries into 4 cm (1½ in) chunks and submerge in the egg mixture. Set aside to soak for 5 minutes.

Grease a 22 cm (8¾ in) oval or round baking dish with the butter and sprinkle a thin layer of sugar over the top.

Spoon the egg mixture into the dish and bake for 35–45 minutes, until the top begins to colour and a skewer inserted into the centre of the pudding comes out clean.

POMES AL MAHÓN

Mahón-stuffed apples

SERVES 4

'Queso Mahón' is a young, creamy, well-rounded cheddar-type cheese. It's named after the port of Mahón in Menorca, where the British brought across cattle for cheese production during their occupation in the 18th century.

Mahón cheese has a salty, tangy and mineral taste due to the high sea salt content in the local grass pastures. It's ripened in caves for as little as two months for young cheese and up to 12 months for the salty, drier and harder Mahón reserva.

This dessert ticks all the boxes when you can't decide between a cheese board, fruit platter or baked sweet.

20 g (¾ oz) unsalted butter, softened
4 apples
120 g (4½ oz) aged Mahón reserva or 12 month-aged cheddar, grated
2 thyme sprigs, leaves finely chopped
sea salt flakes and freshly ground black pepper
1 tablespoon Calvados or brandy
10 hazelnuts, roasted, skinned, roughly chopped

Preheat the oven to 180°C (350°F) fan-forced. Grease a small baking tray with the butter and line with baking paper.

Slice one-quarter off the top of each apple and remove the core, being careful not to core all the way through.

Gently spoon out the apple flesh, leaving a 5 mm (¼ in) layer of apple behind. Place the apple flesh in a bowl with the cheese and thyme and season with salt and pepper. Mix well to combine and smash up any larger apple chunks using the back of a fork. Set aside in the fridge for 10 minutes.

Sprinkle 1 teaspoon of Calvados or brandy into each hollowed-out apple and stuff to the top with the cheese mixture. Transfer the stuffed apples to the prepared tray and sprinkle over the hazelnuts. Bake for 15–20 minutes, until the cheese is melted and bubbling.

Serve with a drizzle of the remaining juices in the baking tray.

FLAM DE TARONJA

Orange custard caramel

SERVES 4–6

In Spanish, flan refers to the French crème caramel. Both countries compete for the origin of this dish; however, the French tend to make individual portions of this wobbly-set custard, while the Spanish go large! This sophisticated flan has a hint of almond extract, which pairs really well with the orange. It's simple to make, but it's worth starting the day before and letting it set overnight in the fridge, to mellow out the eggy flavour.

4 oranges, finely zested
juice of ½ orange
220 g (8 oz) caster (superfine) sugar
500 ml (17 fl oz/2 cups) full-cream (whole) milk
1 cinnamon stick, broken in half
3 large free-range eggs
3 free-range egg yolks
¼ teaspoon almond extract
boiling water

Preheat the oven to 160°C (320°F) fan-forced. Place a 23 cm (9 in) oval baking dish in a large deep roasting tin.

Combine the orange zest and juice in a small bowl and set aside for 5–10 minutes.

Heat half the caster sugar and 3 tablespoons of water in a small saucepan over medium–high heat and gently swirl the pan for 3–4 minutes, until the sugar turns a golden caramel colour. Pour the caramel into the base of the baking dish.

Gently warm the milk, cinnamon and orange zest liquid in a saucepan over medium–low heat until just starting to simmer. Remove from the heat and set aside to cool a little.

Whisk the eggs, egg yolks and almond extract in a large bowl, then add the remaining caster sugar and whisk until creamy and pale.

Strain the orange milk into the egg mixture, whisking to combine.

Pour the custard into the baking dish, then pour enough boiling water into the roasting tin to come halfway up the side of the dish. Bake for 40–50 minutes, until the egg is just set and still a little wobbly in the centre. Gently shake the tin – if the flan is firm around the edge but still has a slight wobble in the middle, it's ready (it will continue to cook as it cools).

Remove the tin from the oven and carefully transfer the baking dish to a wire rack to cool for 30–40 minutes. Refrigerate overnight to chill and allow the egg to completely set and mellow in flavour.

To unmould, run a sharp knife around the edge of the caramel, then invert onto a lipped serving plate. (The trick is to expose the caramel to air. Once this happens, it will slide out quickly so be ready to catch it.)

Take one of the zested oranges and slice off the top and bottom. Place the orange flat on a chopping board and, using a sharp knife, slice off the peel and white pith. Slice into the orange either side of each segment and gently pull the segments to release them.

Scatter the orange segments over the caramel and serve with some sweet pedro ximénez sherry on the side.

GREIXONERA DE BROSSAT

Baked ricotta cheesecake

SERVES 6

The burnt Basque cheesecake may have a cult following around the world, but this humble Balearic version sticks to the original ingredient – ricotta – instead of the modern supermarket cream cheese. Mixing the cream and ricotta together essentially creates a homemade version of cream cheese, except without any gelatine or other thickening agents. The locals also don't burn their version – well not on purpose anyway!

Historically an Easter dessert, this ricotta cheesecake is now eaten all year round throughout Spain as the household's go-to quick weeknight dessert if the kids deserve a treat. I sometimes make smaller portions of this in ramekins, or even miniature ones are great, too. It's also freezer-friendly if you need a bribery tool for unruly children!

20 g (¾ oz) unsalted butter, softened
500 g (1 lb 2 oz) full-cream (whole milk) firm ricotta
125 ml (4 fl oz/½ cup) thick (double/heavy) cream
6 large free-range eggs, beaten
250 g (9 oz) caster (superfine) sugar
zest of ¼ lemon, plus extra to serve

Preheat the oven to 180°C (350°F) fan-forced.

Grease a 25 cm (10 in) round earthenware or ovenproof dish with the butter.

Using a fork, mix the ricotta and cream in a large bowl until smooth. Slowly pour in the beaten egg and whisk until well combined and you can't see any lumps. Add the sugar and lemon zest and whisk until smooth.

Spoon the mixture into the prepared dish and bake for 35–40 minutes, until golden and a skewer inserted into the centre of the cheesecake comes out clean. Alternatively, if you want to serve it Basque-style, cook for 50–60 minutes, until the top is dark brown and almost burnt at the edge.

Sprinkle over a little extra lemon zest and serve with some fresh fruit on a hot day. Perfect!

MACARRONS DE SANT JOAN

Saint John's 'pasta pudding'

SERVES 6

In Ibiza, this dessert is synonymous with the midsummer celebration of Sant Joan at the end of June. There's even a small white-washed village called Sant Joan de Labritja.

This pasta-based version of rice pudding was originally made to use up homemade pasta before the heat of summer spoiled the batch. It used to be served with water, as milk was considered a luxury, but thankfully, nowadays, milk is the standard, which makes this a much creamier and more delicate treat. Today it's made using the specially named short wide-ribboned pasta 'Sant Joan', which is similar to the Italian 'mafaldine corte' or 'reginette' (little queens) pasta. I like to think a pirate from Sardinia or Corsica threw his pasta overboard back in the looting days and it floated its way to Ibizan shores.

1 litre (34 fl oz/4 cups) full-cream (whole) milk
2 cinnamon sticks
peel of ½ lemon, white pith removed, plus lemon
    zest to serve
peel of ½ orange, white pith removed
300 g (10½ oz) caster (superfine) sugar
250 g (9 oz) mafaldine pasta, broken into 4 cm (1¼ in) lengths

Gently warm the milk, one of the cinnamon sticks, the citrus peels and sugar in a large saucepan over medium–low heat until just about to simmer.

Bring a large saucepan of salted water to the boil and cook the pasta for 2–3 minutes, until just cooked on the outside, but still raw on the inside. Drain and add to the warm milk. Cook for 6–8 minutes, until the pasta is al dente.

Evenly divide the pasta among six ramekins, discarding the cinnamon and peel. Set aside to cool slightly, then refrigerate for at least 4 hours or, ideally, overnight.

To serve, finely grate the remaining cinnamon stick with a microplane over each portion and finish with a sprinkling of lemon zest.

FLAÒ EIVISSENC

Ibizan tart

SERVES 6–8

This is the king – King Jaume I if you want to be specific – of desserts in Ibiza and you won't leave the island without having eaten a few servings of this moreish emblematic cheesecake. This recipe comes from Es Torrent, a secluded unspoilt beach of pebbles surrounded by cliffs. Punters travel there by boat courtesy of the Es Torrent restaurant, where they lunch far away from the clubs and party hotspots on the island.

200 g (7 oz/1⅓ cups) plain (all-purpose) flour, plus extra for dusting
1 tablespoon caster (superfine) sugar
¼ teaspoon fine sea salt
2 teaspoons aniseed, bruised in a mortar and pestle
120 g (4½ oz) cold unsalted butter, plus extra for greasing
1 free-range egg yolk
1 tablespoon olive oil
2 tablespoons granulated raw sugar

Mint and goat's cheese filling
4 large free-range eggs
250 g (9 oz) caster (superfine) sugar
200 g (7 oz) cream cheese
200 g (7 oz) cottage cheese
100 g (3½ oz) goat's curd
2 mint sprigs, leaves finely chopped

DESSERTS

Place the flour, sugar, salt and aniseed in a large bowl and rub through the butter with your fingertips until the mixture resembles breadcrumbs.

Combine the egg yolk and oil in a small bowl, then add to the flour mixture and bring together to form a rough dough. Transfer to a lightly floured work surface and lightly knead the dough until you have a smooth, round ball.

Place the dough ball between two sheets of baking paper and gently flatten into a thick disc. Refrigerate for 20–30 minutes.

Grease a 23 cm (9 in) flan (tart) tin with a little butter. Roll the dough out to a 4 mm (¼ in) thick circle. Peel off the top layer of baking paper, then lightly flour the rolling pin and drape the pastry sheet over the pin, so the remaining baking paper is facing upwards. Gently lay the pastry in the prepared tin and peel off the other piece of baking paper. Gently press the pastry evenly into the side of the tin (work quickly so the pastry doesn't soften). Place in the fridge for 40–60 minutes to firm up.

Preheat the oven to 180°C (350°F) fan-forced.

To make the filling, lightly beat the eggs and caster sugar in a bowl. In a separate bowl, combine the cheeses, then gradually add the egg mixture and whisk until combined. Stir through the chopped mint leaves, then spoon the mixture into the pastry case. Cut off any overhanging pastry, then transfer to the oven and bake for 50 minutes or until lightly golden on top.

Sprinkle the raw sugar over the tart and set aside to cool before serving.

GREIXONERA DE CARBASSA

Pumpkin pie

SERVES 6

In Mallorca and Ibiza, 'greixonera' is the name of the terracotta dish used to bake many cakes and desserts. Now substituted for a springform cake tin or a Teflon-coated baking dish, this traditional pumpkin pie, originally from Menorca, is also made with potato or sweet potato as well as savoury versions containing cheese and sobrassada.

You will still find a lot of grandmas out there making it the traditional way and if you have a 'greixonera' it is well worth using it, as the heat is even and takes time to reach the inside of the pie, giving a wonderful thick crust to baking.

1 kg (2 lb 3 oz) butternut pumpkin (squash), peeled, deseeded and chopped into large chunks
100 g (3½ oz) salted butter, melted then cooled, plus extra for greasing
180 g (6½ oz) caster (superfine) sugar
3 free-range eggs, lightly beaten
½ teaspoon ground cinnamon
zest and juice of ½ lemon, plus extra sliced lemon to serve
vanilla ice cream or custard, to serve

Steam or microwave the pumpkin for 6–8 minutes, until soft and cooked through. Set aside in a colander for 30 minutes to drain as much liquid as possible.

Preheat the oven to 150°C (300°F) fan-forced. Grease a 26 x 17 x 3.5 cm (10¼ x 6¾ x 1½ in) brownie tin or similar-sized earthenware dish with butter.

Press out any remaining liquid from the pumpkin and place it in a large bowl with the butter, sugar, egg, cinnamon and lemon zest and juice. Mash everything together until you have a smooth, homogenised batter. Spoon the batter into the prepared tin or dish and cook for 1 hour on the bottom shelf of your oven.

Serve with slices of lemon for squeezing over and some vanilla ice cream or custard spooned over the top.

TORTE DE LLIMÓN

Lemon meringue tart

SERVES 8–10

The British left this dish behind in Menorca and it's now a favourite in households and pastry shops. It's made with a cookie base and sweetened condensed milk – none of that French sweet pastry and cream bother, although they do turn to France for the meringue.

150 g (5½ oz) unsalted butter, softened, plus extra for greasing
375 g (12½ oz) plain milk cookies, such as Marie or Nice
pinch of sea salt flakes
4 large free-range eggs, yolks and whites separated
120 ml (4 fl oz) freshly squeezed lemon juice
zest of 1 lemon
395 g (13½ oz) tin sweetened condensed milk
½ teaspoon cream of tartar
250 g (9 oz/2 cups) pure icing (confectioners') sugar

Preheat the oven to 180°C (350°F) fan-forced.

Grease a fluted 25 x 5.5 cm (10 x 2¼ in) round flan (tart) tin with a removable base with a little butter.

Place the cookies in a large bowl and crush using the end of a rolling pin or the base of a small bowl. Alternatively, for a finer result, blitz the cookies in a food processor. Stir through the butter, salt and 2 tablespoons of warm water until evenly combined, then transfer the mixture to the base of the prepared tin. Using the base of a glass, evenly press the mixture into the base and side of the tin, then set aside in the fridge for 30 minutes to firm up.

Bake the tart shell for 10 minutes or until just beginning to brown around the edge. Remove from the oven and set aside to cool on a wire rack.

Using a hand-held whisk or a stand mixer, whisk the egg yolks, lemon juice and zest and the condensed milk until creamy and combined. Pour into the cooled tart shell and bake for 15 minutes or until lightly set. Set aside to cool on a wire rack, then refrigerate for 1–2 hours, until completely set.

Measure 250 g (9 oz/1 cup) of the egg whites into a clean, dry bowl and whisk using a stand mixer or electric beaters on medium–low speed until soft peaks form. Increase the speed to high, add the cream of tartar and gradually add the sugar, 1 tablespoon at a time, in a slow, steady stream until incorporated and the meringue is thick, glossy and stays standing when you lift out the whisk.

Transfer the meringue to a piping bag and pipe it onto the top of the set lemon tart in any design you like.

Preheat a grill (broiler) to medium. Grill the tart on the middle shelf until starting to colour or use a blow torch to slightly burn the surface of the meringue.

Slice and serve!

QUARTOS EMBETUMATS

Layered sponge and meringue cake

MAKES 6 SINGLE-SERVE CAKES

Mainly found in and around the bakeries of Palma, these heavenly, sweet, fluffy white cakes most famously come out of the ovens at the Can Frasquet pastry shop in the Mallorcan capital. The cakes consist of a simple sponge (coca de quart) filled with a cured egg yolk custard (or sugared yolks), that are then enveloped in Italian meringue! The chocolate glaze is optional – some people prefer it without, but I feel it's needed to balance the sweet meringue, plus it adds another layer of texture, which I love.

A little Mallorcan trick to prevent the sponge from sinking is to drop the tin on the floor when you take it out the oven to knock the cake into line!

10 free-range eggs, separated
100 g (3½ oz) cornflour (cornstarch) or
    potato flour, plus extra for dusting
400 g (14 oz) pure icing (confectioners') sugar
100 g (3½ oz) caster (superfine) sugar
¼ teaspoon cream of tartar

Chocolate glaze
260 g (9 oz) dark chocolate (70% cocoa solids),
    finely chopped
120 g (4½ oz) unsalted butter, melted,
    plus extra for greasing
3 tablespoons corn syrup

Preheat the oven to 150°C (300°F) fan-forced. Lightly grease a lined 24 x 17 cm (9½ x 6¾ in) cake tin with butter and lightly dust with flour.

Place six egg yolks, the cornflour and 100 g (3½ oz) of the icing sugar in a large bowl and whisk to create a well-combined batter. Set aside.

Place the six egg whites in the bowl of a stand mixer and beat on medium–low speed until stiff peaks form. Gently fold the egg whites into the egg yolk mixture until evenly mixed through. Pour the cake batter into the prepared tin and bake for 30 minutes.

Remove from the oven and drop the cake tin flat on a hard-surfaced floor to help prevent it sinking. Set aside on a wire rack to completely cool, then turn the cake out and slice horizontally in half.

Heat the caster sugar and 100 ml (3½ fl oz) of water in a small saucepan over low heat until the sugar is dissolved. Allow to cool completely, then stir through the remaining egg yolks. Return to a low heat and stir continuously for 6–10 minutes, until the mixture thickens to a custard and coats the back of a spoon. Set aside to cool.

Heat the remaining icing sugar and 250 ml (8½ fl oz/1 cup) of water in a saucepan over medium heat. Bring to a simmer and cook for 12 minutes or until the sugar reaches the soft-ball stage (110°C/230°F on a kitchen thermometer).

Meanwhile, beat the remaining egg whites in the bowl of a stand mixer on medium speed until frothy. Add the cream of tartar and continue to whisk until soft peaks form. With the mixer set to medium–high speed, slowly and carefully pour in the hot sugar syrup in a thin, steady stream. Keep beating until you have stiff and glossy peaks.

Spread the custard over one of the cut sponge halves and top with the other half. Cut into six even rectangles.

To make the chocolate glaze, melt the chocolate in a bowl set over a saucepan of simmering water. Stir through the melted butter and corn syrup and transfer to a jug for easy pouring.

Using a spatula, coat the cakes in the meringue evenly on all sides. Transfer to serving plates, pour the chocolate glaze over the top and serve.

PONX D'OUS

Eggnog

SERVES 6

From the English word 'punch', this traditional British Christmas egg–milk punch is served at carnivals, fiestas, balls and other grand occasions throughout the Balearics, but particularly on Menorca where the culture of drinking dark rum was left behind by British soldiers returning from fighting in America.

Choose a good-quality, spiced dark rum for this cocktail.

500 ml (17 fl oz/2 cups) full-cream (whole) milk
250 ml (8½ fl oz/1 cup) thick (double/heavy) cream
1 cinnamon stick
1 strip of lemon peel, white pith removed
½ teaspoon vanilla bean paste
½ teaspoon freshly grated nutmeg
5 egg yolks
110 g (4 oz/½ cup) granulated sugar
185 ml (6 fl oz/¾ cup) dark rum
60 ml (2 fl oz/¼ cup) brandy

Combine the milk, cream, cinnamon, lemon peel, vanilla and half the nutmeg in a saucepan over medium heat and bring to a gentle simmer. Remove from the heat and set aside to steep for 10 minutes, then strain into a jug.

Using a stand mixer or electric beaters, whisk the egg yolks, then beat in the sugar until thick and pale. Gradually pour the infused hot milk into the egg mixture, whisking constantly until completely combined. Return the mixture to a clean saucepan and add the rum and brandy.

Gently warm over low heat for 3–5 minutes, until the eggnog thickens slightly, stirring to avoid scrambling the egg.

Remove from the heat and set aside to cool, then either refrigerate to serve later or serve at room temperature with the remaining nutmeg dusted on top.

TAMBOR D'AMETLLA

Almond and caramel nougat praline

MAKES 500 G (1 LB 2 OZ)

In Spain, anything sweet, stuck together and moulded is called a 'turrón'. The closest we have to it is nougat, but this is more of a whole praline that's served in large pieces (not like the French with their small, shattered-glass accompaniment). Each region of Spain has their own specialty nougat and this one proudly hails from the Spanish islands.

You can find this praline at winter markets and Christmas fairs, cooking in large cauldrons over wood fires and being stirred to a rich, dark honey colour before being set in hot trays and cut while warm into large rectangular slabs. It will certainly give your jaw a workout!

200 g (7 oz) blanched almonds
200 g (7 oz) raw almonds
400 g (14 oz) caster (superfine) sugar
25 g (1 oz) unsalted butter
½ lemon

Preheat the oven to 180°C (350°F) fan-forced.

Spread the blanched and raw almonds in a single layer on baking trays and bake for 8 minutes or until toasted. Set aside and keep warm.

Line a baking tray with baking paper or use a silicon mat and place it in the oven.

Gently warm the sugar and 2 tablespoons of water in a saucepan over medium–low heat until about half the sugar has dissolved, then add the warm almonds. Stir constantly with a wooden spoon, until the sugar begins to caramelise and darken, then remove the pan from the heat and spread onto the hot baking tray or silicon mat, working quickly to spread while hot, to a 2 mm (¹⁄₁₆ in) thickness. Use the lemon half, cut side down, to smooth over the top of the praline slab. Cut the praline while still warm if you prefer regular shapes. Alternatively wait for it to cool and snap into large shards.

Wrap the praline in baking paper and store in an airtight container for up to 3 weeks. It also makes a great gift, wrapped in colourful string.

Menorcan nougat

Almond and
caramel nougat
praline

Nougat cake

Eggnog

COCA DE TORRÓ

Nougat cake

MAKES 3 CAKES

This round Christmas nougat, also known as soft Mallorcan nougat, is quite similar to marzipan but not as strong. Shaping it is fun and it's super simple to make, requiring no cooking or baking. It's the perfect gift to take when visiting relatives or friends for the festive season.

500 g (1 lb 2 oz) blanched almonds
boiling water
25 g (1 oz) butter
400 g (14 oz) pure icing (confectioners') sugar
zest and juice of 1 orange
⅓ teaspoon ground cinnamon
6 large edible rice paper sheets, cut into 16–18 cm (6¼–7 in) rounds

Place the almonds in a heatproof bowl and pour over boiling water to cover. Set aside for 2–3 minutes, then drain the almonds and blitz in a food processor to a smooth paste. Add the remaining ingredients, except for the rice paper, and blitz until well combined. Roll the almond mixture into three even-sized balls.

Lay a few sheets of plastic wrap on a work surface and place a sheet of rice paper, rough side down, on top. Place one almond ball in the centre of the circle and place another paper circle directly on top. Using an ever-so-slightly damp tea towel, press down gently but firmly to spread the nougat into the shape of the rice paper. Leave a 2 mm (¹⁄₁₆ in) border around the edge, then wet the border and stick it to the side of the nougat cake, so it's completely enveloped in the paper. Repeat with the remaining nougat and rice paper sheets to make three cakes.

Slice into triangles and serve.

The nougat cake will keep in an airtight container for 7–10 days.

CUSCUSSÓ

Menorcan nougat

MAKES 600 G (1 LB 5 OZ)

Menorcans' love for sweets is a legacy left behind from the Moors who occupied the island more than one thousand years ago. They also left names of villages starting in Bini (son of), along with Moorish bath houses over in Palma de Mallorca.

Named after the grain couscous, this traditional Christmas sweet typically comprises not much more than breadcrumbs, almonds, butter, dried fruit and nuts.

I like to use left-over croissants or ensaïmadas instead of bread if I have them on hand, which means I don't need to add any butter, making this a very quick and easy process made with ingredients you probably already have in your pantry.

200 g (7 oz) blanched almonds or ground almonds
250 g (9 oz) left-over Ensaïmadas (see page 32), croissants or brioche bread
100 g (3½ oz) candied mixed fruit mix (such as pear, pineapple, orange, fig, cherry)
100 g (3½ oz) pure icing (confectioners') sugar
1 tablespoon honey
50 ml (1¾ fl oz) freshly squeezed orange juice
¼ teaspoon ground cinnamon
zest of ½ lemon
20 g (¾ oz) pine nuts, lightly toasted
30 g (1 oz/¼ cup) raisins
30 g (1 oz/¼ cup) walnuts, chopped

If using blanched almonds, blitz them in a food processor to a fine crumb. You can skip this step if using ground almonds, just tip it into the food processor. Add the pastries and candied fruit and pulse together to form a paste.

Place the sugar, honey and orange juice in a saucepan and bring to the boil over medium heat until the sugar has dissolved. Remove from the heat and stir through the cinnamon and lemon zest.

With the motor running, gradually pour the orange syrup into the food processor until combined, then add the pine nuts and raisins and pulse to distribute evenly through the mix.

Place a 35 cm (14 in) square of foil on a work surface and top with a sheet of baking paper the same size. Spoon the nougat mixture along the centre of the paper, then roll up the baking paper and foil into a tight log. Twist the ends to seal, then refrigerate for 2–3 hours to set.

Slice into 1 cm (½ in) thick discs and serve with a scattering of chopped walnuts.

GRÀCIES

For my second book, I would like to thank the following people who dared to come with me on this ride again so soon after my first book, *The Catalan Kitchen*.

Morgan – thank you for being the best, caring, understanding, loving and involved partner in my life, along with our son, baby Hector and Doodles the dog.

The whole Smith Street Books crew who are such a dedicated bunch of independent and funky book creatives. I'm super proud to be a part of your growing family. Paul McNally, publisher and founder of Smith Street Books – thanks for giving me another book, for trusting in my content and enabling this special body of work to come to life. Lucy Heaver, my publisher and friend, once again this book is our love-child and we make such gorgeous babies! Thank you for your guided direction, experience, knowledge and support, but above all, thank you for your honesty, always.

Evi O, designer – thanks for connecting with me and this special place in the world to make these pages come alive with style, inspiration and imagination.

Heather Menzies, typesetter – I'm very privileged to have had your expert eyes again bringing it all together.

Helena Holmgren, indexer – seriously, thank you again! I admire the incredible work you do putting everything in order.

Rochelle Eagle, photographer – your commitment to this work and constant focus on the best outcome always keeps me in check. Thanks for coming on board with everything you've got (and more!) for round two of more Mediterranean adventures!

Lee Blaylock, stylist – thanks for saying yes again, for going above and beyond on this project and for being proud of what we do.

Josh Nicholson-Reekie – it's great to be around you, as I can always be myself. Thank you for your help on the shoot, for cooking and for organising me every day. I'm very grateful for all your personal support and comradery over the years.

Meryl Batlle – Guapisima! Thanks so much for your professionalism and global understanding of 'les illes Balears'. Thanks also for your drive and passion for the art of living and transmitting so much into this project, including your crepes!

Suppliers – thank you for giving me guidance and always having time for me in our busy worlds. Thank you to Gary and Ash McBean, the Narduzzo family at Pino's, Stella from D&J Chickens and all the ladies at Essential Ingredient, along with families and staff who are all so passionate. Special thanks to Kino at El Colmado for your continuing generosity, dedication to Spanish products and improving our reach to these special ingredients. Thanks also to La Central Deli & Bodega at South Melbourne Market for your support.

Personally – thanks to my mother, Beverley, and father, Keith, and their partners Michael and Robyn. Thanks also to Sue and Neil for being there when I needed you most and for being such invaluable, irreplaceable grandparents. This would all be impossible without you all to lean on. My oldest buddies Anna Frances and Eleanor Jean – thanks for making me feel like a superwoman while at the same time telling me I'm not. My eclectic soulmates Samantha Lane, Emma Bulpit, Martina Tuohey, Jason and Jose, Emma Rudin, Georgina Konstandakopoulos and Thomas John – thank you so much! Karen Martini and Matt Preston – thank you for your ongoing encouragement and for always barracking for me.

My Balearic families – thanks to Julia for being there on the other side of the world for some midnight tennis texting. Gràcies to the Saunders/Cumberlege tribe at The Sea Club, Mallorca, for having me all those years and showing me so much about this wonderful part of the world. Also thanks to the people in Ibiza who trusted me, helped me and backed me. You know who you are. It was a tough ride, but we have unforgettable memories for life.

Moltes Merces a tots!

INDEX

Smith Street Books

Published in 2019 by Smith Street Books
Melbourne | Australia
smithstreetbooks.com

ISBN: 978-1-925811-26-1

Publisher: Lucy Heaver
Project editor: Lucy Heaver, Tusk studio
Art Director: Evi-O.Studio | Evi O.
Designers: Evi-O.Studio | Evi O., Susan Le and Rosie Whelan
Typesetter: Heather Menzies, Studio 31 Graphics
Photographer: Rochelle Eagle
Stylist: Lee Blaylock
Food preparation: Emma Warren, Meryl Batlle and Josh Nicholson
Printed & bound in China by C&C Offset Printing Co., Ltd.

Book 104
10 9 8 7 6 5 4 3 2 1